You want fries
with that?

You want fries that?

a collection

with

Ken Hoffman

Winedale Publishing
Houston

PUBLISHED BY WINEDALE PUBLISHING CO.

Distributed by the Texas A&M University Press Consortium

Library of Congress Cataloging-in-Publication Data
Hoffman, Ken, 1950-
You want fries with that? / by Ken Hoffman
p. cm.
ISBN 0—965—7468—5—2
1. Food habits—Humor.
2. Popular culture—Humor.
3. Travel—Humor.
PN6231.F66H64   1999
814'.54—dc21   99-34877   CIP

Manufactured in the United States of America
First Edition

Book Design by Kellye Sanford
Illustrations by Howard Sherman

To the guests on the Jerry Springer Show,
who make me feel a whole lot better about myself.

Contents

Acknowledgments

My wife Erin and our little boy Andrew; Jack Loftis and Susan Bischoff of the *Houston Chronicle*; Sherry Adams in the *Chronicle* library who dug up all these columns; Diamond Dallas Page, Sonny Drysdale, Matty Alou, Lenny Davidson, Alvy Singer, and the editor of this book, Babette Fraser.

And to all the workers in the drive-through who never get my order right, who hand me Dr. Pepper instead of Diet Coke, who forget the napkins, who give me double the mustard instead of ketchup only . . . I'll get even with you someday.

Introduction

I've always had fun with my newspaper column.

It's allowed me to do things and go places and meet people I never dreamed of.

I've whacked tennis balls with Bjorn Borg and John McEnroe and Chris Evert. I scored five points for the Washington Generals against the Harlem Globetrotters. I've shagged fly balls with my boyhood hero Willie Mays. I have been bodyslammed by too many professional wrestlers to count.

I've slept, huddled under animal skins, in a teepee near the Arctic Circle, and counted the stars in the Australian sky. I've traveled to the Orient to meet the greatest inventor of the twentieth century. No, not some computer geek. The man who invented the Whoopee Cushion and Dribble Glass.

I've been around the world upside and down. I've been to Russia and Cuba and Vietnam and backstage at the *David Letterman Show*. I made my TV acting debut in the last episode of *M*A*S*H*. Don't blink. I was there when the Berlin Wall came down. On the show *Cheers*, if you look real close at the pay phone on the wall, I scribbled, "Diane, call Ken Hoffman, it's important."

I shook hands with four presidents and John Lennon.

Along the way, by accident really, I became the No. 1, most-read restaurant critic in America. My food reviews run in newspapers across the country. They're read by millions.

Yet I know absolutely nothing about food.

I'm not surprised so many people read my reviews, though. That's because I write about restaurants where so many people eat. I

1

am the "Drive-Thru Gourmet." I specialize in restaurants that serve food that's bad for you.

I haven't seen a tablecloth in years.

This book is a collection of my columns from the *Houston Chronicle* and, before it closed, the *Houston Post*. These are the ones I had the most fun writing.

I've tried to mix them up, some columns about my travels, the people I've met and the hamburgers I've eaten.

Most of the columns are pretty much as they appeared in the newspaper, plus a few longer pieces. One of the longer stories is about infertility and trying to have a baby. That one wasn't fun. Funny, I hope. But fun? No.

But at least it has a happy ending. My beautiful little boy Andrew just turned two.

1. _____

"You Will Get a Baby."

It's Not a Lot of Laughs

I can't conceive . . . of a more embarrassing situation.

I'm flat on my back on a doctor's ice-cold examining table, wearing one of those absurd hospital gowns that tie in the back so your rear end hangs out. No underpants. My knees are bent, legs spread.

They're spread so a female radiologist has clear access to my private parts. She's examining them with a sonogram instrument that looks like the microphone Wayne Newton uses in Las Vegas.

I'm uncomfortable and embarrassed. I'd rather be anyplace else in the world, except maybe Las Vegas at a Wayne Newton concert.

It occurs to me that the radiologist is looking at parts of my body I haven't seen in years. While this is going on, I'm watching live pictures of my testicles on a TV monitor next to the examining table. Talk about your Kodak moments.

I should explain here that I wasn't having these photos taken for the Hoffman family album. To be honest, I was doing it for the opposite reason. There isn't a Hoffman family album.

That's the whole problem. I can't conceive.

My wife and I haven't been able to get pregnant.

After a few years of trying normal measures, if standing on your head after intercourse is normal, we went to a doctor who specializes in fertility problems. Soon we were pinpointing the best days, hours and minutes. This resulted in frantic phone calls at the worst times. "Come home right away, my temperature is 99.2, Venus is aligned with Mars, and Ed Brandon said there's a thirty percent chance of precipitation!"

We got silly suggestions, such as, "Drink cough medicine." We put statues of ancient fertility gods next to our bed. I changed my

7

diet. I switched to boxer shorts. We tried everything. And nothing worked.

When even the boxer shorts failed, my wife went in for a quicky medical once-over. She passed.

Then it was my turn. Which is how I got on this table watching a TV show starring my genitals. I hate going to the doctor for normal stuff. I'm always afraid he'll find something horribly wrong and pronounce me dead right there on the spot. Just as soon as I pay the bill.

This is so humiliating. Plus, this little photo shoot is costing me $300.

On top of that, the radiologist isn't even my type.

I'm not a fertility expert (although my private parts play one on TV). To me, it's Buck-Rogers-in-the-twenty-fifth-century advanced biology. All I know is that a total stranger was zapping me with sound waves and checking for varicocele, which are tiny veins that raise the temperature of your testicles and foul up the whole sperm factory.

My testicles were fine.

The next step, three flights up, was to have my prostate examined and photographed. Cindy Crawford never had this many photos taken in one day. I had my prostate photographed front, back and sideways. It's too excruciating to describe, but let's say that now I know what the puppet Lambchop feels like when Shari Lewis gets through with him.

My prostate was fine, too. "Not enlarged, nice and smooth," the doctor said. He raved about it so much, I almost asked him for a wallet-size photo.

That way, when people asked whether I had any children, I could say, "No, but would you like to see a picture of my prostate? Cute little fellow, isn't he?"

Since my wife and I checked out okay, the doctor suggested we begin a program of mild fertility drugs. These were pills designed to kick-start her ovaries so she'd produce more eggs. We had to keep a chart of her basal body temperature. It looked like Frank Billingsley's hurricane tracking chart.

The pills didn't work.

At the time, it didn't bother me too much that we weren't getting pregnant. It just wasn't that big a deal to me. It was to my wife, though. She's more serious about these kinds of things. She grew up in an Ozzie-and-Harriet kind of home and had an extremely normal childhood. I didn't.

She threw herself into getting pregnant. It became her mission. Every book she read had a title like *Conquering Infertility* or *How to Have a Baby When the Doctor Says You Can't*. When we watched TV and a scene with a baby came on, I hit the channel-changer as fast as I could. It made her too sad. All of her friends having babies didn't help, either.

On my side of our bed, I have a dresser with two drawers. The top drawer used to hold my socks and underwear. They were kicked out in favor of books about infertility. My socks and stuff went into the bathroom, under the sink, next to the plunger. There's a pleasant image.

She got frustrated and sad. I got frustrated and made jokes. Everybody deals with disappointment differently.

But eventually my attitude toward having a baby changed. I began feeling that I was ready, too.

As I found out, relationships aren't easy when you're trying to get pregnant and can't. Our doctor warned us about this. He said there would be tension, that we might blame each other even though we know it's nobody's fault.

I also had a tough job situation last year that didn't make me a joy to be around. Now there were two cranky people in the house. Little disagreements became major issues. It drove me crazy when Channel Thirty-nine moved its *Seinfeld* reruns from ten p.m. to six p.m. What were those guys thinking? Thank goodness they came to their senses and put *Seinfeld* back on at ten.

A while later, our doctor advised us to begin taking more powerful fertility drugs. You sometimes read about these drugs when a woman in Mongolia gives birth to an entire city. Multiple births are not uncommon. Suddenly I was the Nutty Professor, mixing vials of drugs and unwrapping a fresh hypodermic needle. These drugs, we were told, have a success rate of about fifteen percent to twenty percent. Not great odds.

For ten nights each month, my wife would grab onto the bathroom sink, drop her drawers and take a deep breath, and I'd give her a shot.

How would you like to turn around and see someone like me holding a needle? No way I'd do it.

As shots go, it's better to give than to receive. But not a whole lot better. Sometimes I'd hit a vein and leave an ugly black-and-blue mark on her rear end. There's another pleasant image.

It's not a lot of laughs not getting pregnant.

By the way, I always thought it was impossible or illegal to buy hypodermic needles. I thought the government didn't want drug addicts getting them. Nonsense. My wife bought huge boxes of them at the drugstore. No prescription. No note from the doctor. They're about twenty-five cents each.

Still nothing. Each month she'd buy a home pregnancy test, and each time it would come up negative. Then she'd visit the doctor's office for a blood test that would confirm no pregnancy.

These fertility drugs are expensive, and insurance doesn't cover them. That's when I made a drug run to Mexico, to the lovely border town of Nuevo Laredo. In the United States, each dose of fertility drugs costs about $55. In Mexico, it's about $18. It's worth the trip. Plus there's a twelve-year-old kid in Nuevo Laredo who'll write your name on a grain of rice for $1. I'm convinced I could make a fortune with this kid in the United States.

Thousands of Americans routinely walk across the bridge from Laredo to Nuevo Laredo to buy drugs they either can't get or can't afford at home. I stood in line at a farmacia behind Americans buying three-month supplies (the legal limit) of Valium, diet pills, steroids and who-knows-what-else, and I picked up my fertility drugs.

A woman from Houston recognized me and asked what I was buying. I was too embarrassed to say fertility drugs, so I said I was just getting some toothpaste.

I drove six hours for toothpaste, that's what I told her.

Back in Houston, I had to visit a clinic several times to get my sperm tested. There is no delicate way to describe this procedure. Here goes: They put you in a room. They give you a dirty magazine and a little plastic cup. Then you go for the gold.

The nurse always had a cute word for this chore, like "collecting" or "harvesting."

Over the past two years I harvested so many times I could have been the opening act at Willie Nelson's Farm Aid concert.

As things developed, my wife and I were both a little responsible for our nonpregnancy.

The doctors discovered that she had endometriosis, a common condition that blocks sperm from its job. She had laser surgery to clear it up. Then she took more drugs to shut down her reproductive system for three months while she healed.

My sperm, we learned, had low motility. I had an acceptable number of sperm, but they weren't about to make the U.S. Olympic swim team.

Separately, each of us could become a parent with no sweat. With other people. Together, though, we were in trouble.

By this time I was reading all those infertility books in my sock drawer. One article said the sperm count of the average American man has declined by half over the past century. Another article suggested it might be because of environmental pollution or food additives. So about a year ago, I tried becoming a vegetarian.

I never got that right, either. I wasn't a vegetarian so much as I just didn't eat meat. For two months I ate whole chocolate-covered banana cakes for breakfast. I put away ice cream by the quart. I ate family-size bags of potato chips. But no meat. I gained ten pounds as the world's worst vegetarian.

But you know something? My sperm count did go up. Enough for us to begin artificial insemination. Back to the clinic for some more collecting.

Let me explain this collecting business. It's not as much fun as you might remember from high school. I'm not a whiner, but I've seen TV shows such as *Mad About You* and *Coach* and movies such as *Forget Paris*, and those guys had it a lot better than I did. In *Forget Paris*, they put Billy Crystal into a room with a VCR, a comfortable recliner and a healthy stack of porno tapes.

That's Hollywood. My room at the clinic was a tiny bathroom with a sink, a toilet bowl and a hard plastic chair. No dirty movies. Just a few crumpled copies of *Playboy* and *Penthouse*. The magazines were so old I expected the centerfold to be Zsa Zsa Gabor.

It's so cramped in there, you have to be Pretzel Boy to keep everything where it belongs.

I remember one bizarre collecting experience. Usually our artificial-insemination sessions were in the middle of the week, and we were the only couple scheduled that hour. One time, though, we had to go on a Sunday morning, to a different clinic. There were five other couples in the waiting room. Nobody said a word to nobody. Nobody had to. We were all therefor the same lousy reason. As Debra Winger said in *Forget Paris*, "You could cut the hopelessness with a knife."

Before I continue, there's another thing: When you go to collect, there's a sign-up sheet at the window where you turn in your specimen. I always scribbled my name lefty so nobody could read it.

One day I saw a Houston TV newscaster's name on the sheet. He'd written his name as if he were signing an autograph.

To me, this was nuclear ammunition. I couldn't wait to call him and say, "Oh, by the way, you do anything interesting today?" And then let him have it good. (Meanwhile, he got the last laugh. He and his wife are pregnant. We're not.)

Anyway, back to my Sunday appointment. Instead of letting us sneak in and out, they called three names at the same time and showed us to three separate rooms. Again, not to complain, but this place didn't supply dirty magazines.

The only magazine I had was a *Newsweek* from the waiting room.

I'm a pretty competitive person. I saw this as a contest. No way was I leaving my room first.

I sat in there with my *Newsweek* and read a story about the Republicans' chances in the upcoming election. I read a movie review, a story about the Cleveland Indians and letters to the editor. I thought about writing a letter to the editor myself. Like, "How come you don't publish photos of naked women?"

Fifteen minutes went by, and I figured I was home safe. I put the *Newsweek* away, got down to business and emerged with my plastic cup.

I was the first one out.

I was stunned. I looked at the wives sitting there and yelled, "I won!" My wife buried her head in her hands.

On the way home, she explained how much embarrassment I had caused her and what an idiot I was. As if I'd never heard that lecture before.

We tried the fertility injections and artificial-insemination routine four times. Last month, we came up empty again. We met with our doctor, who began his well-practiced speech with, "We've reached a crossroads."

It was like being called into the principal's office to get yelled at. Just get it over and let me out of here.

I broke in—politely, I thought—and said: "This isn't working, and I don't think it ever is going to work. We'd like to talk to you about adoption."

Needless to say, I got another lecture from my wife on the way home. Although we had agreed on the adoption route, she said I should have let the doctor finish his speech.

Our doctor is one of the best in the business at helping couples deal with fertility problems. From start to finish, he was understanding, sympathetic and totally supportive. He understood. He's got a tough job. His patients try their brains out to get pregnant, and the odds are stacked against them. I felt just as sorry for him each time we didn't get pregnant.

My reading list changed immediately to books about adoption. The doctor gave us a thick folder packed with names of adoption agencies and people in Houston who've adopted children.

I have several friends who have adopted. Some of the children came from the United States, others from China and Guatemala.

I wondered about adopting a child from Russia, because back in the Stone Age, that's where my family came from. But we're concentrating on the United States for now.

I've read and heard so much about adoption, and I have such a good feeling about it, that if I were given a magical choice between us getting pregnant and adopting a child, I probably would pick adoption.

Every one of my friends who's adopted a child says the same thing: "There is absolutely no difference between holding your adopted child and a child you conceived yourself. The adopted child is just as much yours."

Of course, this is just my situation. Other couples go on taking fertility drugs for ten years. Sometimes they wind up getting pregnant and everything turns out great.

But I'm tired of home pregnancy tests coming up negative. I'm tired of mixing drugs and sticking my wife with needles. I'm tired of driving to Mexico. I'm tired of being yelled at. I'm even tired of those visits to the doctor's bathroom with a *Playboy* magazine, although I must admit I was getting pretty good at it.

But mostly, I . . . we . . . are tired of being disappointed.

Recently we went to an orientation session at an adoption center. We learned about the various ways of adopting, from agency-assisted to designated to international adoptions. We learned about the legal end of adoption. We talked with several birth mothers and adoptive parents.

The president of the adoption center met with about thirty couples and said: "We know you've all been through a trying experience. But I can tell you one thing: If you are approved, you will get a baby. We are going to help you get a baby, and it will happen."

It was the first encouraging thing I'd heard in two years.

Now, if you'll excuse me, I have about fifty pages of adoption applications to fill out. And I've got to get the house cleaned. I understand the adoption-center folks make several visits to your home, and they can be pretty thorough.

First thing, I have to get my socks out from under the sink.

2

"I'm Trying to Eat."

Worse than a Wig

One night last week, around four a.m., I stumbled downstairs for some Diet Pepsi and got one of the scariest shocks of my life.

Just as I was taking a swig straight out of the bottle (who's looking at that time of night?), the light from the refrigerator revealed a hideous pile of fuzzy fur on the kitchen floor.

Now I'm used to seeing disgusting clumps of fur inside the refrigerator. I've got fruit in there that looks like ZZ Top. I have green and blue bread with enough penicillin to open a Walgreen's. I've got eggs that archaeologists would be frightened to crack open.

I'm no stranger to UFO's—unidentified furry objects.

But never on the kitchen floor.

What could this ugly, frightening mess of unruly hair be? A rabid raccoon? Marv Albert's wig?

No, worse.

It was a cat.

A greedy fat cat had squeezed through my dog door and was eating Sophie's and Lilly's leftovers in their dishes. I screamed like a banshee, hitting an octave the great Beverly Sills would envy. The cat looked at me as if to say, "Could you keep it down? I'm trying to eat."

Great—on top of scaring me to death, he's got an attitude.

I threw the closest weapon of mass destruction I could find—a wet dishrag—at him. He calmly walked to the dog door, squeezed his fat carcass through it, and bounded off into the night.

How long has this been going on?

I want it stopped.

I'm not a cat person. Cats give me the willies. It's bad enough they jump over the fence and poop in my bushes. I don't want this cat visiting me all hours of the night. Especially if he doesn't call first. And it would kill him to bring a cake once in a while?

The same thing happened the next night.

The cat was back.

I can't let this continue. It's time for action. I'm going after this cat like Bill Murray chasing the gopher in *Caddyshack*. I would never hurt an animal, but I want him out of my life.

The first thing people said was, "How come your dogs don't take care of the problem? If anything tried to eat my dog's food, he'd bite them faster than Mike Tyson."

My dogs sleep upstairs with me. They don't budge. Burglars could break into my house and cart off everything I own, and the dogs wouldn't lift a paw. As long as burglars leave the bed, they're fine. Watchdogs they're not.

It's up to me to handle the problem. I was advised to wait in the dark, and when the cat sneaks in, shoot a water pistol at him. Cats hate to get wet.

This sounds like a good idea. I've got nothing else to do all night. And I do own a black ski cap. I'd have to go buy gloves, though.

Another person told me to start leaving him crummy cat food. He'll go searching for better grub.

Somebody else said I should buy a Dog Door 2000, which opens and closes by a radar device attached to my dogs' collars.

I've got a better idea. How about if my neighbor keeps his cat on his own property? Like the law says he's supposed to. Yeah, that'll happen.

I've decided to hire the Adopt-a-Cat group to apprehend my cat burglar. These people do it all the time. Their M.O.: I should put a bowl of cat food outside my house like I'm running a drive-through. Then each night, move the bowl farther away. Once I have him far enough away, the Adopt-a-Cat group will set a trap.

They'll even come, take the cat and find him a new home with a nice family in a different neighborhood.

So starting tonight, it's a feline movable feast. I've got a nice bag of Meow Mix ready to go.

Here, kitty, kitty.

And don't forget to stop at the post office for some change of address cards.

Plumbing Heroes

From Day One, my bathtub took a couple of hours to drain. It was very annoying. It looked bad. It didn't smell so terrific, either. So I called a plumber, an expensive one with a quarter-page ad in the Yellow Pages.

Right on schedule, in a shiny, just-washed truck, wearing a freshly starched uniform, the plumber arrived. He poured a vile potion down the drain. Dreamer, I thought.

I already had tried every supermarket-approved drain opener. Drano, Liquid Plumm'r (regular and professional strength). I tried Red Devil lye.

The plumber tried snaking my drain. That didn't work, either.

He went outside, looked on the roof and discovered the problem. My bathtub drain didn't have a vent. It was a structural defect, from when the house was built in 1950. The bathtub probably always took hours to drain, he said.

I simply needed a few new pipes, a contraption and a vent. I didn't understand a word he said. Then he gave me an estimate for $300 and a bill for $100.

A hundred dollars for what? You didn't fix my tub.

I complained to the plumbing company. They sent another plumber who confirmed the first plumber's diagnosis. My tub needed $300 worth of fixing.

For $300 I'll stand in a foot of water. For $300 I'll stand knee-deep in the muddy Mississippi.

That was more than a year ago.

Last week I sprung a gas leak and needed a plumber again. I asked a Realtor friend if he knew a good plumber.

"Call my guys. They're real good and cheap. Just don't expect them to show up in suits and ties."

They were late. Their truck was a dusty heap. They were Larry, Darryl and Darryl from the Newhart show. But they fixed my gas leak in five minutes. The bill was only $30.

"While you're here, could you check the bathtub? The drain doesn't drain."

I figured maybe these guys will do it for $250. "I need a few new pipes, a contraption and a vent."

They ignored my expert diagnosis and fiddled behind the tub.

"You have a vent. It's vented through the commode. It's hard to see, but it's there," Larry said.

Larry filled the tub, hopped in and started plunging like he was making butter. Darryl blew (yuck) on a pipe. The other Darryl stuffed rags into the faucet.

Water splashed everywhere. It sounded like walrus mating season. My bathroom looked like free admission day at Wet 'n' Wild theme park.

Suddenly . . . thwack!

Something, a blur, erupted from the drain and smacked against the wall. It was a big, bristly, stinky, old-fashioned shaving brush. The kind Floyd the barber used on Andy Griffith.

"From the looks of this, I'll bet it's been stuck down there for forty years," Larry guessed.

While we marveled at the brush, I glanced at the tub. Hey look, the water's gone.

"You should see the stuff we get out of drains. I've seen rats, wallets, pantyhose, books, you name it," Larry said.

I turned on the water just to watch it go down. This is great. I can take a shower without my feet getting crinkly.

And I saved $300!

It's Impolite to Point

There are three basic rules at a nudist resort.

1) No pointing.

2) No staring.

3) And definitely no laughing.

"Otherwise, just relax, lay back and enjoy your day in the country. Sunbathing in the nude is the best way to get rid of those unsightly tan lines," said Linda Krabill, general manager of the Live Oak Nudist Resort in Washington, fourteen miles east of Brenham, Texas.

Saturday afternoon I visited Live Oak during its open house in honor of National Nude Weekend. The nude helicopter ride was enough to lure me out there.

Actually, there are two more honest-to-goodness rules:

4) Everybody must sit on a towel. It's for hygiene.

5) Although people rarely do, you're allowed to wear clothes, especially if it gets chilly. The only place you absolutely, positively must be nude is in the pool.

With 700 members, Live Oak is the largest nudist resort—don't you dare call it a "colony"—in Texas.

It looks like a regular resort. Live Oak has a pool, cabins, a restaurant called Bare Delights, recreation facilities, a clubhouse and souvenir shop.

For children, there's a Goofy Kidfest, with a Slip 'n' Slide covered with chocolate pudding.

Yes, everything looks regular.

Except nobody's wearing clothes. And that includes the kids.

The guy pouring me a lemonade: Naked.

The woman screaming "Bingo" in the game room: Nothing on.

The woman strumming a guitar: Not a stitch.

I did not get naked with them. I don't even walk around naked in front of my dogs. If I'm alone in the house, and I use the bathroom, I close the door.

I think I look horrible naked. You think I'm going to play volleyball nude in front of total strangers, most of whom have worse bodies than I do?

"We aren't hung up on appearance. We have all ages, shapes and sizes here. We don't place importance on that," Krabill said.

The first naked adult I ever saw was a photo of a woman in a nudist resort magazine. She was playing volleyball.

"Back in the '30s and '40s, when nudist resorts got popular, they didn't have a lot of money. Volleyball was a cheap sport to play. Nudists became associated with volleyball and it's still our favorite sport," Krabill said.

Saturday was ninety-five degrees with a scorching sun. How come they don't burn their feet in the sand?

"It's a little trick we do," Krabill said. "We constantly water down the sand."

And how come everybody isn't sunburned to a crisp? Aren't they worried about the harmful effects of the sun?

"In the early days of nudist resorts, it was about sun worshipping. Now it's more about the freedom of the lifestyle," Krabill said.

"People stay out of the sun, or they use sun block. In fact, I'm going to start regular visits by dermatologists who'll educate people about skin cancer and check those who wish to be looked at. I'm going to call it 'The Mole Patrol.' With nudists, it's easy to check them out."

Nudists are honest folks. There isn't a clerk at the souvenir store.

"We stock T-shirts, books, videos, candy bars, suntan oil, Blue Bell ice cream—all the essentials of life," Krabill said.

Customers pick an item and, later on, pay for it at the office.

"If you dropped a $100 bill, somebody would pick it up and

bring it to the lost and found," Krabill said. "This isn't a good place for thieves."

Particularly pickpockets.

Is That You, Arto?

NEAR THE ARCTIC CIRCLE, FINLAND—I am cold and wet and cranky. I'm wide awake, wrapped like a mummy in reindeer hides, inside a *kota*, a Finnish teepee that leaks.

Shhhh. I think I just heard a bear. These woods, ten miles from the Russian frontier, are crawling with them.

Wild animals are starting to play a big role in my life. For dinner, I had venison stew. I'm not complaining. As food chains go, I say give me venison. The night before, I ate half a plate of chopped beaver before they told me what it was.

Tonight I'm sharing a teepee with two guys I met only a few days ago. One is telling how he got started as a writer. The other guy is sound asleep, snoring like a buzz saw.

I envy the guy snoring.

We've been fishing and hiking and white water rafting and doing lots of nature things I'm no good at. Dinner was cooked by a real-life burly mountain man named Arto. He's got a bushy red beard. His pants have a special loop for carrying hunting knives.

Around nine p.m., most of the group I'm with trudged back to the lodge. Three dopes stayed.

Steve is from New York City. He lives in a three-room apartment. "The closest I've come to wildlife in the past five years is killing cockroaches in my apartment," he said. I'm not Daniel Boone, either. To me, "roughing it" is when my cable goes out.

The other guy is Bruce, from Linden, N.J., right next to my hometown of Elizabeth. He has no business sleeping in the woods, either.

I asked Arto if it'll be too cold to sleep outside. Nah, he sleeps out here in the dead of winter, when the temperature hits thirty below.

Tonight the weather will be balmy, barely touching freezing. We'll be fine, he said.

We each grabbed a couple of reindeer skins and made a bed in the teepee. Reindeer skins are cheap, only $10 for the whole carcass, because they shed so much. Before this week, I figured I might see a live reindeer in Finland. Now I'm cuddled up inside two dead ones.

Oh, good, they left the heads on.

Arto said to build a small fire inside the teepee to stay warm. I went to the woodshed and got enough logs to build a shopping mall. I built a blaze that sent smoke signals to Moscow.

Back at the lodge, they're drinking and yakking away in the bar. I'm praying that wasn't a bear I just heard.

I brought along a pocket radio and tried to tune in something. I wonder if they have call-in talk shows in Russia.

Larry Kingovitch: "We have a call from Staskosova, what's your question?"

Caller: "Do you think the free market system will work and HOWARD STERNSKY RULES!"

There wasn't a single station on AM or FM.

Aha! Arto left his cellular phone on the picnic table. I dialed the AT&T code for America. Got right through. I didn't talk long, though.

I was scared to death of Arto, anyway. That's all I need, him catching me dressed like Bullwinkle Moose and making international calls on his phone.

In a few hours, it will be daybreak and we'll hike to the lodge. We'll be covered with loose reindeer fur. On our shirts, down our pants, sticking in our mouths like reindeer hairballs. Smoke, stew and wet reindeer fur. Now there's an attractive cologne.

At breakfast, others from our group will ask how our night went.

"It was the best! You missed the greatest experience of the whole trip," we'll say.

Then I'm going to bed. Alone. With no reindeer.

Look, But Don't Eat

Bam! The second the camera blinks off for a commercial, that's when things really heat up on "*Emeril Live!*," America's Number One cooking show on the TV Food Network.

Emeril's assistants race onstage to finish cooking what Emeril started; a makeup artist dusts the shiny perspiration off his nose; food carts are wheeled on and off the set; crumbs from the last dish are swept away and ingredients for the next are laid out; Emeril wanders into the audience and leads a conga line of children to the freezer for ice-cream cones and Oreo cookies.

All the while, a booming sound system plays, believe it or not, disco music and Partridge Family hits from the '70s.

"*Emeril Live!*" may be the hottest ticket in town. So many foodies hunger to watch chef Emeril Lagasse in action that the Food Network had to set up a lottery system for tickets.

The small studio holds barely a hundred people. More than a quarter million fans mailed in for tickets.

The show is called "*Emeril Live!*" because he cooks in front of an audience, but it's on tape. Emeril flies to New York six times a year to knock out shows faster than a microwave oven. He tapes as many as four hourlong programs in a day. Bam! Bam! Bam! Bam!

I attended an "*Emeril Live!*" taping last week.

Fans lined up two hours early outside Metropolitan Studios on 106th Street and Lexington, in not the nicest part of New York City. They chatted excitedly, "What do you think he'll be cooking?"

"Think we'll get any?"

I thought, with my luck it'll be hamburgers and french fries.

Before the taping started, a stage manager laid down some rules:

No autographs, no sunglasses, no hats and no chewing gum. "You don't want to look like a cow on TV," he said.

And the Rule of Rules: "Food may be passed out during a commercial. Be nice to the person sitting next to you. Share the food. But whatever you do, don't eat anything until we come back from commercial. We want the people at home to see you enjoying the food."

A lucky handful of guests—maybe twenty—get to sit at small tables directly in front of the cooking area. They're safely within arm's reach of Emeril, which means he may pass them some food.

The rest of the audience sits on folding chairs in the peanut gallery. They won't be eating today.

For this show, it's really the macadamia nut gallery. Emeril is devoting the hour to Hawaiian cuisine. He's going to make coconut fried shrimp, fried plantains, mango chutney, pineapple cream pie and, with the help of Hawaiian chef Sam Choy, mahi mahi fingers encrusted in nuts. The show is scheduled to air in mid-April.

I hit the jackpot. I was seated at Table Four, right in front of the stove. I could feel the heat from the burners. On *Emeril Live*, this is a power table.

Everybody in the audience was given a souvenir pineapple, which we were told to wave each time Emeril said the word "pineapple." We also got a small pack of nuts, the size you get on Southwest Airlines.

Emeril demonstrated how to make the batter for coconut fried shrimp, and threw a few in the deep fryer. During a commercial, an assistant finished battering and cooking the rest of the shrimp. Small samples were passed to my table.

Oops. I started eating the shrimp. I forgot about waiting for the commercial to end. Excuse me, but when the most famous chef in America gives me free food, my instinct is to put it right in my mouth.

I was busted. A stage manager ran at me with his arms waving.

He practically made me spit it out. "No, wait for the cameras," he said sternly.

I also got to sample the mahi mahi fingers. I told you I had a power table. The mahi mahi looked like fish sticks, but they sure didn't taste like Mrs. Paul's.

This time I waited for the cameras, but I broke a different rule. I forgot to share the food with my neighbor.

Except I didn't really forget.

I figured, I'll never see this person again. Let him eat Mrs. Paul's.

Pillow Talk

I'm not a good sleeper. When I wake up, sometimes the pillow is halfway across the room, I'm sweating like Rodney Dangerfield, I can't find one sock and my clock radio is not tuned to the same station it was when I went to bed.

That's why I had to try Dr. Watanabe's Sobakawa Pillow, the "original Oriental sleeping secret." As seen on TV.

The Sobakawa Pillow infomercial is hosted by "sleep expert" Dr. Kazu Watanabe and former Suzanne Somers wannabe Jennilee Harrison. Back in 1980, when Somers demanded a huge salary increase for her fine acting on *Three's Company*, the producers booted her off the set and hired Harrison as their scab ditzy blonde.

Thank goodness everybody came to their senses a year later. Somers was back on *Three's Company*, tickling America's funnybone, and Harrison was soon sent packing.

The Sobakawa Pillow costs $29.95, and if you order right away, they'll include a nifty Lone Ranger mask that supposedly eliminates puffiness around your eyes.

The Sobakawa Pillow isn't stuffed with feathers or foam like normal pillows you buy on sale at Target. No, the Sobakawa is packed with 100-percent Grade A premium buckwheat hulls. It's like a Beanie Baby for your head.

Why buckwheat hulls? If you've seen the infomercial, you know that buckwheat won't burn. Set a match to feathers or foam, and you can break out the marshmallows. But buckwheat? Not a spark.

It's comforting to know that your whole house can burn to the ground, and when the insurance adjustor trudges through the charred remains, your Sobakawa Pillow will be in mint condition.

The Sobakawa Pillow is small. It's only fourteen inches wide and eight inches long. That's about the size of a pillow you get on airplanes, only with less B.O. and drool stains.

I have two big problems with this pillow. One, it's loud. Every time you move your head, it sounds like the world's biggest bag of Orville Redenbacher at full blast in a microwave oven.

The Sobakawa is sort of hard, too. It isn't fluffy and soft where your head sinks in. With the Sobakawa, you stay aloft. Dr. Watanabe says that's support. I say that's sleeping on rocks.

But hey, if worse comes to worst, you can rip open the Sobakawa and boil up those buckwheat hulls. They're excellent with macaroni. In a Jewish deli, this is called kasha and bow ties. Don't forget a nice piece of cheesecake to go.

The Sobakawa Pillow is designed for back and side sleepers. It is not recommended for stomach dozers like me. I have never seen myself in a ceiling mirror. I wonder what I look like sleeping?

Stomach sleepers need special pillows. Fortunately, pillow technology provides us with uncommonly flat and extra cushy headrests. Of course, they stick us for a buck extra per pillow.

At times in my life, I've tossed my pillow in the closet altogether. Slept like a baby, too. I saved a fortune on pillowcases, too, but I felt like a dummy whenever a good pillow fight broke out. Like on my honeymoon.

The Sobakawa Pillow does keep your head a few degrees cooler than feathers and foam. A chilly noggin is essential to the Asian theory of "Su-Kan-Soku-Netsu," which says we function better when our head is cool and our feet are warm. In Japan, people routinely keep their tootsies toasty at night.

I'm there, dude. I've always worn socks to bed. It's a very sexy look.

Here's where the Sobakawa Pillow gets completely ridiculous, though. They actually put an instructions sheet in the box.

"Duh, honey, can you help me figure out how to use this thing? It looks pretty complicated."

Let me guess: 1. Put pillow on bed. 2. Put head on pillow. 3. Close eyes.

On the other hand, if you're buying a beanbag stuffed with a kosher side dish from an infomercial for $29.95, maybe you do need instructions on how to use a pillow.

Free the Animals

Elephants do not look good in sequins.

Monkeys, given a choice, would not dress like bellboys and go roller-skating.

Tigers don't wake up and say, "It's crazy, but I'm in the mood for jumping through a blazing hoop while some geek threatens me with a whip."

The circus would be much more fun if they got rid of the animals.

Last week I went to the Ringling Bros. and Barnum & Bailey Circus. I entered through the garage.

I walked past elephants chained at the foot and tigers locked in cages. I don't know what a happy-go-lucky elephant looks like, but this wasn't it.

During the circus, they paraded the elephants in a circle. Each elephant wrapped its trunk around the tail of the elephant in front. That's a dangerous place to be.

While an acrobat did somersaults on its back, one elephant decided this was the perfect time to go to the bathroom. It was like Mount St. Helens and Old Faithful rolled into one. The first ten rows instantly reeked.

This is fun?

There is something about a man with a whip and frightened animals that I can't watch.

Dog acts are fine. Prancing horses are interesting. These animals are easily trained and enjoy the work. But wild animals, like tigers and lions, belong in the wild.

Ringling Bros. says the circus is celebrating its 200th anniversary in the United States, and animal acts have always been a part of the circus. Animal acts are a tradition.

It's time to drop this tradition. Or Ringling Bros. may discover itself facing a new tradition—empty seats. The circus was less than half-filled the night I went.

It would be good business to lose the animal acts. It costs a fortune to keep elephants on the road. They eat hundreds and hundreds of pounds of food a week. How do you think they produce all that elephant doody the circus gives away as fertilizer?

Human performers are far more entertaining than animals, anyway. Give me a good contortionist over a phony-baloney unicorn any day.

Clowns are funny. Dancing bears are pathetic.

I'm not against all performing animals. I think Stupid Pet Tricks on *David Letterman* is great. That's because I imagine the dogs on Stupid Pet Tricks go home, watch themselves on TV and sleep in bed with their owners.

Tigers in the circus sleep in cages.

Besides, traditions come and go. Attitudes toward animals have changed. Dog fighting used to be a tradition.

Now people want cosmetics that aren't tested on animals. When tourists go on African safari, they're more likely to shoot a camera than a gun. Zoos are built without cages.

People love animals. The circus brags how its animals are well treated. They have a licensed veterinarian nearby at all times. But are circus animals loved?

I happen to think the Houston Livestock Show and Rodeo would be just as popular if they eliminated one or two rodeo events, like calf-roping, where the cowboy picks up a baby cow and body slams it like Hulk Hogan.

Fifty thousand fans come to hear Garth Brooks. They aren't there to watch "Pecos Pete" dig his spurs into a steer so he'll jump higher.

The Livestock Show is terrific, although I'll never understand why they have to kill the Grand Champion steer. If I were a steer, I'd bribe the judges to pick somebody else.

Avoid Gypsies

ROME—My vacation in Europe was going great, just like the book said, on less than $40 a day.

I bought a $318 round-trip ticket to Paris. I climbed the Eiffel Tower, ate a Quarter Pounder on the Champs Elysée, saw the Madonna movie in Nice, gawked at topless women on the beach in St. Tropez, got yelled at for taking a snapshot, and rode a motor scooter to Monaco.

I played the slot machines in Monte Carlo, ate a pizza in Naples, watched the Italian Open tennis tournament, ate more pizza in Rome, and tossed a few thousand worthless lira in Trevi Fountain.

Then, on my last day in Rome, a guy who needed a shave waved a gun at a bunch of us, screamed something in Italian, and threw us off the No. 64 bus to Vatican City.

It's the little things that can ruin a vacation.

Yesterday I was eating a hot fudge sundae on Princess Grace Avenue. Today I'm pinned against a building, scared to death, while a guy is screaming in Italian. The Pope goes on at noon; I'm going to miss him, I just know it.

And I'm not mingling with such nice people. My back was to the wall with three men who look like extras from *Godfather III*, a couple of gypsy women, my buddy Jake, and an overweight tourist who's screaming bloody murder in German. I wish somebody would scream in English for a change. Suddenly the Madonna movie didn't seem so bad.

The Italian screamer separated me and Jake from the others. "Non comprende vous Italiano," I told him. "English? *Anglais?*"

He didn't speak English.

Now I'm playing charades and Pictionary with a guy with a gun on the sidewalks of Rome.

He was a cop. A young hip undercover cop who rides the buses arresting pickpockets. And he's pretty sure that one of the gypsy women dipped into Jake's pants. He was right. "My wallet is gone!" Jake said.

They didn't get my wallet. I, the veteran tourist, hide my money so well that Kreskin couldn't find it. But this was Jake's first time in Europe. Pickpockets were taking numbers like in a bakery to see who nailed him.

Jake should have known better. That morning we took a tour and the guide warned, "We have many pickpockets. Be careful of gypsy women and their children. The mother will try to sell you something and their children will steal from you."

This was the last day of our trip, so there wasn't much in Jake's wallet. A couple of dollars, a few francs, some lira and a credit card pleading for mercy. The German man was hit harder. From his gestures, he'll be hitchhiking back to Hamburg.

I'm halfway around the world, and tourists are taking photos of us. "This is the Roman Coliseum—click—here's the Pantheon—click—and here's a slide of two Americans getting arrested in Italy."

We went to the police station. Two hundred thousand tourists are in St. Peter's Square being blessed by the Pope, and we're studying a police lineup, trying to pick our gypsy woman from a bunch of Corporal Klinger look-alikes.

It was easy. I recognized her clothes. Because it was a hot day, she wore only six sweaters and a thick blanket.

At least we were dealing with a detective who understood English.

"That's her. Frisk her, wash your hands thoroughly, give Jake his wallet and thanks for everything but we must be going."

"We cannot do that."

"Why cannot you do that?" The detective spoke better broken English than I did.

"She must have a lawyer."

Finally I said, "We have a train to catch. Here is our address. If you find Jake's wallet somewhere, anywhere on this woman, just mail it to America. You guys are wonderful. I thought Robert De Niro deserved the Oscar. Bye."

No wallet yet. Frisking a gypsy can take weeks.

Miss Kim Proposes

"Listen, a traditional Korean haircut is wild. It's like a geisha house, aerobics studio and PTL Club all rolled into one. When you leave that barber shop, I promise you'll feel like Superman!"

My friend, an engineer for NBC Sports, had been in Korea for several months. It's a wonder he wasn't bald.

So I got a haircut in Korea, halfway around the world, without a reservation, without a coupon from Randalls.

"They're not going to speak English," the engineer advised. "But whatever they ask you, trust me, just say yes."

I took a cab deep into the heart of Seoul, not the best part of town, but I've stumbled around in worse.

There was a red and white striped pole outside the barber shop. There were three young ladies, three chairs (no waiting) and one old man inside.

My hostess, Miss Kim, was about twenty-two, thin, and a sharp looker despite an angry spread of pimples on her chin. She introduced me to my barber, Mr. Park. The Koreans are fine, hard-working folks, but they need more names. They're all named Kim, Park or Lee. Sure it's easy to buy monogrammed shirts, but try looking somebody up in the phone book.

Using charades and a photograph of Jay Leno, I begged him to take nothing off the top, and leave the sides and back alone.

While Mr. Park snipped the air above my head, Miss Kim draped my legs over a table and nudged my feet into a sink. To make things easy on both of us, she washed my feet. I don't know this person's first name and she's got my feet all sudsy. What's love got to do with it, got to do with it?

Then she rolled up my pants and massaged my legs. She kneaded me much too hard. For fifteen minutes, I thought I was wrestling Mrs. Baird.

She tugged and yanked and pulled on my arms. She gave me everything short of an Indian rope burn. She threw boiling hot, steaming towels on me. She judo chopped me. She grabbed my fingers, one at a time, and cracked my knuckles. There goes my bowling average.

Meantime, Mr. Park is snipping and clipping. He pinched me with his scissors. I checked for blood. I would have complained but he doesn't understand English. And besides, Miss Kim is removing my shirt.

I am now sitting in a mysteriously dark, funky-smelling Korean barber shop, a million miles from home, with no shoes, socks or shirt on. And the torture is, I have to watch this in a full-length mirror.

I've got to do some sit-ups.

And where's my wallet?

Miss Kim is rubbing my shoulders, softly now, and I feel wonderful.

The barber finishes my imaginary haircut and vanishes. It's just Miss Kim and me, and I'm half-naked.

Miss Kim orders me to lie down on my stomach. She throws one leg over and climbs aboard. She's Willie Shoemaker and I'm Seattle Slew. She pounds me down the backstretch and gives me the massage of my life. Wake me when *Cheers* comes on. All I need is a Neil Diamond record and I'm asking Miss Kim to the prom.

Miss Kim flips me over again, and blindfolds me with a hotel towel. She's rubbing and squeezing—and I can't see a thing. I'm uncomfortable and scared now. What if Miss Kim slipped out and I'm getting rub-a-dub-dubbed by her drunken uncle Mr. Lee?

"Shaving?" she asks.

"Yes," I say. I have never been shaved by anyone else, except once by a nurse, and I tried everything to avoid that nightmare. Miss

Kim wraps my face in a towel that is so hot you could roast frank-furters over it. I feel like screaming, but I don't want to ruin the whole *M*A*S*H* effect.

Miss Kim uses an old-fashioned straight-edged razor. I remember the NBC engineer saying, "It's terrific, but it's a little weird the first time she presses that blade against your neck."

She shaves my forehead and the edges of my ears. What is this, Eddie Munster Day in Korea?

Miss Kim is nice. Miss Kim is attentive. Miss Kim is strong.

Most of all, Miss Kim could use a breath mint.

Miss Kim tried to give me a full frontal massage but I declined. I'm saving myself for a haircut back home.

She finished me off with a manicure. She drilled a Q-tip so deeply into my ears that Roto-Rooter filed an infringement of copy-right suit. She gushed water into my nose and ears.

The bill was $30 with tipping prohibited. I slipped Miss Kim an extra $5. I figured I'd probably need another haircut tomorrow.

A Pig Sandwich

This week I reached out for a Pig Sandwich . . . and a slice of fast-food history at the Pig Stand restaurant, near downtown Houston.

Here's the blueprint: about six ounces of sliced slow-smoked pork loin, topped with sour-pickle relish and barbecue sauce on a toasted hamburger bun. Total calories: 585. Fat grams: 26.

The Pig Stand chain, which opened in 1921, was the birthplace of the drive-through window. Richard Kirby, the original owner, is said to have thought, "People with cars are so lazy they don't want to get out of them to eat!"

What a visionary!

Kirby was not, however, the first man to ask, "You want fries with that?"

Everything else pretty much did start at the Pig Stand.

It offered the first drive-in curb service. Waiters would hop on cars' running boards and take customers' orders. That's how they got the name carhops.

The Pig Stand invented fried onion rings, the chicken-fried steak sandwich and Texas toast.

The Pig Stand is to fast food what Cooperstown, N.Y., is to baseball. It's where it all started. And both places have nifty souvenir shops.

The signature dish is, of course, the Pig Sandwich.

Each morning, even before the breakfast waitresses get there, Pig Stand cooks throw enormous ten- to fifteen-pound pork loins into the smoker. The loins spend all day soaking up smoky Texas mesquite flavor. The result is the tenderest, juiciest, leanest pork you'll ever eat.

The first Texas Pig Stand was in Dallas. The idea of eating in your car immediately captured the imagination of Texans and other Southern folk.

Within a decade, there were Pig Stands across the South, some sixty restaurants from Florida to Southern California, all with the simple slogan "Eat a Pig Sandwich." Bright flashing Pig Stand signs (yes, they were among the first to use neon) popped up overnight.

History happened with regularity and often by mistake. Fried onion rings were invented when a cook accidentally dropped some raw onion slices into a bowl of chicken-fried steak batter. He threw them into the deep fryer to see if they'd be any good. They were.

Texas toast was created when a Pig Stand ordered a local bakery to slice its bread a little thicker than normal. The slices wouldn't fit into the toaster. So the cook buttered both sides of the extra-big bread and warmed them on the griddle.

Big bread. Big state. Texas toast.

During the Great Depression of the 1930s, many Pig Stands, including the original Dallas site, disappeared just as quickly as they had sprung up a decade earlier.

Today, only seven Pig Stands remain, all in Texas: three in Beaumont, three in San Antonio, one in Houston.

Each one is different, charming in its own nostalgic way.

The Pig Stand on Washington Avenue, which opened in 1924, sports thousands of little pig toys donated by customers.

The restaurant was featured in the movie *The Evening Star*. You can sit in the same booth where Shirley MacLaine scarfed down Pig Sandwiches and chugged milkshakes.

The movie may not have been a hit, but the Pig Sandwiches are still getting standing ovations.

Nice Shot, Chrissie

Last week, women's professional boxer Christy Yaeger smacked me around silly. It was the first time I ever put on boxing gloves. By the end of our match, I was stumbling around the ring like Otis the town drunk on the Andy Griffith Show.

But let the record show, I was still standing at the final bell.

Saturday afternoon, tennis legend Chris Evert delivered the knockout shot. I was seeing stars and Tweety Birds.

I took it on the chin, except it wasn't my chin, at Chuck Norris' "Kick Drugs Out of America" tennis tournament at Westwood Country Club.

It's the premiere tennis charity event in Houston, with former President George Bush, Wimbledon champ Chris Evert, Chuck Norris, Vijay Amritraj, Heisman Trophy winner Herschel Walker and many more celebrities and local media nobodies on hand.

The event raised $400,000 this year, which goes to teach high-risk kids about the discipline of martial arts.

Honestly, I don't care about martial arts. I have no interest in busting bricks with my forehead. I just like to play tennis.

In an early match, Bernie Kopell ("Doc" from the *Love Boat*) and I walloped Walker and Jerry Van Dyke. Kopell's not a bad player; Walker is really fast but doesn't hit the ball hard; Van Dyke is slower than a statue.

My last match was going to be me and tennis pro Anand Amritraj against Evert and Norris. I couldn't wait for that. Evert is an all-time great. Plus, last year she was the announcer during my match against Linda Lorelle, and Evert mocked me for "playing like a girl." It was because I stayed on the baseline and refused to come to the net.

At one point, she called me "Miss Hoffman." All of a sudden, Evert, who used to be known as "The Ice Maiden" for her cold, stoic personality on court, turned into a nightclub comedian. She practically asked the crowd to tip the waiters and "order the prime rib."

So this year, I was going to show Evert just who plays like a girl. I can guarantee that "Doc" and Van Dyke didn't train for the Norris tennis event like I did.

And for once, I didn't choke. Amritraj (my newest and best friend) and I toyed with Evert and Norris. It helped that Norris may be the single most awful tennis player ever.

Norris is a terrific guy. I admire him for donating his time to help Houston kids. And he can rip out my spine with his bare hands. But he's terrible at tennis. During the fifth game of the set, I was serving against Evert and cranked one up. As Emeril Lagasse would say, *bam!* Clean ace. Evert didn't even move on the ball. She just rolled her eyes.

I just aced someone who's won 18 Grand Slam titles (seven French Opens, six U.S. Opens, three Wimbledons, two Australian Opens).

"Miss Hoffman?" Take that, Shecky Evert!

But then again, she does play like a girl.

The match could not have gone better. Amritraj and I were up 5-0, when Evert served the last point.

"Hey, come to the net, you coward. Be a man for once in your life," she yelled at me.

OK, but just once. The match is almost over. I'll do it just to shut her up. She'll serve to Amritraj, and he'll smash it back for a winner. Game. Set. Match. Revenge.

But Evert didn't serve it to Amritraj like she was supposed to. Instead, she smoked it as hard as she could right at me.

Whack! I never saw it coming. The ball hit me right in the . . .

Put it this way: She hit a bull's-eye.

Evert doubled up, gasping with laughter. I just doubled up, gasping.

Hundreds of people in the stands saw the most accurate shot in Evert's career. The whole place was laughing. If she could've hit shots like that, she would have won 118 Grand Slams instead of only 18.

Minutes later, Evert was still laughing. She said to me, "I swear I wasn't trying to hit you, especially not there. You can write that you aced me, passed me twice, humiliated me, disgraced me. I know I'm over the hill when somebody like you aces me. Just make sure you write about that last shot."

I asked her, "How would you like me to describe it? How can I say in a newspaper where you hit me?"

At that point, Bush, once the most powerful man on the planet and leader of the free world, leaned over to me and said, "Say groin. It sounds nicer."

That's just great. Did the former president see my most embarrassing moment?

I finally meet a president of the United States and the only advice he has for me is, "Say groin."

Shrimp Jackpot

Las Vegas is known for two things. Gambling, of course. And bargain shrimp cocktail.

Dirt cheap shrimp cocktail is a tradition in Vegas. The casinos brag about their shrimp. It's there on the marquee, "Shrimp Cocktail 99 cents" next to "Frank Sinatra Jr.—One Night Only."

These aren't big, meaty shrimp, like you find in expensive restaurants. These are tiny critters of incomplete seafood matter. They look like white blood cells under a microscope. You can't eat 'em with a fork, they keep falling through the openings.

One morning recently, ace taste-tester Reg "Third Degree" Burns and I combed downtown Vegas in search of the best and cheapest shrimp cocktail. We visited seven casinos. Six of them had shrimp cocktail at the snack bar. The seventh had a McDonald's.

Third Degree ate 'em, I took notes. Here's our survey.

Golden Gate—This is where it all started. In 1959, owners Italo Ghelfi, Robert Ricardo and Al Durante began selling shrimp cocktail for twenty-five cents. The gimmick quickly spread throughout Las Vegas.

Third Degree, an accountant in his spare time, was impressed. "I counted eighty-four shrimps. The cocktail cost ninety-nine cents plus tax. I found it unusual that some casinos charged tax while others didn't.

"The shrimp came in a heavy-duty ice cream sundae glass with a side of Saltines. It was delicious. Maybe it was because it was my first. My tastebuds are particularly sensitive to shellfish at eight in the morning."

Gold Spike—Third Degree is a purist. He likes his cocktail without frills. No lettuce. No onions. Sauce on the side.

"Hmmm, eighty-one shrimp for fifty cents. That's a bargain. Size-wise, this was the most consistent scoop of shrimp. I may be speaking out of school here, but I believe the shrimp were deveined. The waitress didn't laugh at my jokes, though. So I didn't tip her."

California Club—Mikey didn't like it. The cocktail was served at a Japanese-style sushi bar, perilously close to raw fish. There were only sixty-nine shrimp for a buck. "The cocktail was pre-packaged with lettuce filler," he sniffed.

Plaza—This was your standard Vegas cocktail, sixty-eight shrimp in a shot glass for fifty cents. What sets the Plaza apart was the location of the snack bar, next to the penny slot machines. Where you have penny slots, you have women smoking cigarettes. They had voices deeper than Walter Cronkite.

"It was so smoky in there I almost coughed up a lemon wedge."

Lady Luck—To be fair, Third Degree had eaten a few hundred shrimp by the time we reached Lady Luck. And it wasn't nine a.m. yet.

"At $1.50, this was the most expensive shrimp cocktail in town. I counted 122 shrimp. They tasted very fresh, but I cry foul at the location of the shrimp cart. There was no place to sit and eat, except at a slot machine."

We were dazzled by a sign in the casino: Free slot machine lessons. This is not a complicated process. You put a coin in, you pull the arm, you put another coin in, you go home broke.

Fremont—"The winner! An astounding 210 shrimp for only seventy-five cents! Of course, these were rare pygmy shrimp. I got eye strain counting them. They were less than an eighth of an inch wide," Third Degree said.

Third Degree ate 634 shrimp in less than two hours.

"That's probably the most of anything I ever ate at one time. Peanuts maybe? I don't think so. I was surprised how I didn't get

filled up on the shrimp. On the other hand, I don't think I'll be ordering shrimp again for a long time," he said.

Going the Extra Mile

Last week Continental Airlines offered a terrific deal to members of its frequent flyers club: Two round-trip tickets to Europe for 50,000 miles.

Usually you get one ticket for 50,000.

I called Continental to check how many miles I had. Rats! I had only 49,120. I had to act fast. Frequent flyer deals don't last long.

First I tried to buy the extra miles. Continental sells 1,000 miles for $25.

But since Continental was offering these trips in conjunction with KLM Airlines, buying miles was not allowed. There would be no short cuts. I had to buy a ticket, fly somewhere and get back before Monday morning.

Continental credits 500 miles to frequent flyers no matter how short a flight is. I called reservations and said, "Book me round trip from Houston on the shortest flight you have."

That's Houston Intercontinental to Ellington Air Force Base.

From start to finish, it takes thirteen minutes to cover 24.28 miles. You never leave Houston's city limits.

It's the shortest commercial flight on any airline anywhere in America, according to the Air Transport Association in Washington, D.C.

It's also Continental's cheapest fare. A round-trip ticket is $50.

Actually it's cheaper than that. If you hop aboard at Ellington and connect to another Continental flight at Intercontinental, the trip is free.

Wait, it gets better. Parking is free at Ellington. Considering how expensive parking is at Intercontinental (up to $8 a day), I'm departing from Ellington from now on.

I took the Intercontinental-Ellington turnaround Saturday afternoon. My flight left at 5:01 p.m.

It took one hour to drive my car to Intercontinental. Much to my surprise, there was construction on I-45. I waited in line fifteen minutes to buy a ticket. Then I waited thirty minutes at the gate.

Naturally it was Gate 47, the farthest in the whole airport. I think I walked halfway to Ellington.

All this for a thirteen-minute flight that lands closer to my house than from where I started.

It was a small plane with a propeller. I expected the pilot to wear goggles and a leather jacket.

Elaine, our flight attendant, gave the usual instructions about seatbelts and smoking. Then she sat in the back.

Where's my complimentary peanuts? How about a soft drink? Doesn't Elaine want to know if I'll have the beef or chicken for dinner?

Nothing. Old Mother Hubbard's cupboard had more food in it.

Right after takeoff the pilot came on the loudspeaker.

"Thanks for flying Continental. Sit back and enjoy the flight. By the way, we've been cleared for landing."

Ellington doesn't have a large terminal. Nobody hits you up for donations. There are soda and candy machines and a few pay phones. I called home. It was a local call.

The return flight was just Elaine, me and six other passengers. I barely had time to finish the trivia quiz in the seat pouch magazine.

I didn't know New Zealand was roughly the same size as California. I missed the question about Hawaii, too.

With only thirteen minutes of air time, the plane didn't get too high, only 4,000 feet up. We passed over a softball field. I could have called balls and strikes.

I saw people barbecuing burgers in their back yard.

I landed back at Intercontinental dazed by jet lag. It took another hour to drive home.

But I had my 1,000 frequent flyer miles and I'm off to Europe in May.

Already this is the most expensive free trip I ever took.

Darwin Selects Beer

THE NORTHERN TERRITORY—This town has "gone troppo." That's the Aussie way of saying Darwin's gone plain nuts.

It happens this time every year during "buildup," that sticky stretch leading to the wet season. Each day gets hotter and more humid. The pressure builds. Tempers get frayed. Brains get fried. Beer bottles get opened.

Then Darwin goes kablooey—the annual Hookers' Ball. Three thousand uninhibited people, from teen-agers to city officials, cut loose at the Big Country Saloon last Sunday night.

The dress code is simple: lingerie for the ladies, underpants for men. Accessories optional.

I haven't seen this many whips and chains and tattoos since Cher's opening night at Caesar's Palace.

If you wear undies, admission is only $15. Conservatively attired folks pay $25. A share of the funds go to the AIDS Council of Darwin.

The first Hookers' Ball was thrown twenty years ago by John Spellman, the owner of Darwin's most notorious gay bar. Soon straight people wanted in on the fun.

Now the Hookers' Ball is the highlight of Darwin's social season. It's Australia's most outrageous R-rated event, packed with straights, gays and people who can't seem to decide.

This year's edition was telecast nationally on Australia's largest satellite channel, Sky TV.

Jo Beth Taylor, host of Australia's Funniest Home Videos, was the host.

Rock bands played in two different sections of the Big Country Saloon. They performed in their underpants.

Ever the diligent newshound, I took lots of pictures.

To fully understand the craziness of the Hookers' Ball, you have to look at a map of Australia.

Sydney, Melbourne, Perth, Brisbane and Adelaide are Australia's biggest and most sophisticated cities. They're all to the south, where an occasional cool breeze blows even in summer.

Now head north toward the equator. See that enormous blank space? That's the Northern Territory.

The Northern Territory is two-and-a-half times the size of Texas. Yet only 156,000 people live there. That's a good day at the Houston Livestock Show and Rodeo. It's considered a territory, not a state, because the population is too small.

When you can't go any farther north, you've hit Darwin, the "Top End." Population: 72,000.

It's the beer-drinking capital of Australia.

Until recently, the Swan and Carlton breweries were the biggest industry in Darwin. And still they had to import beer to the city.

In most cities, a "stubby" is a short can of beer holding about eight ounces.

A "Darwin Stubby" is two liters.

"During 'buildup,' nobody in the world drinks more beer than us. It's so hot that you're always thirsty," said Ray Church, bouncer at the Victoria Hotel Pub, one of Darwin's rowdier drinking establishments.

No wonder Darwin is bottoms up. Geographically, it's closer to Malaysia and Singapore than any major city in Australia.

Darwin is Crocodile Dundee country. They have saltwater crocodiles in the Adelaide River that leap out of the water and grab birds.

A popular pub is The Hard Croc Cafe. Another bar has a caged "penalty box" in case of fights.

Next year, McDonald's arrives in Darwin. It should be "troppo" time again. When Burger King opened its first store in Darwin, it broke the Australian record for selling hamburgers.

Who's Smarter?

My dog is a dope.

I love Sophie, but the truth is, she's not very smart. No one would ever confuse her with Lassie when it comes to brains.

Lassie was a genius. She'd run into the barn, bark three times and Timmy could tell a baby was trapped in a boat, the tide was rising and Timmy should bring insulin because the baby is a diabetic. And hurry because a commercial is coming up.

When Sophie barks it means one of two things.

1) She wants a Milk Bone.

2) Someone's ringing the doorbell, but can she have a Milk Bone before I answer the door?

I got Sophie, a Humane Society special, about four years ago. She's part-golden retriever, part-cocker spaniel, part God-only-knows.

When she buries a brand new, overpriced rawhide toy in the back yard, it's a goner. Sophie couldn't find it again with a treasure map, night vision goggles and a Geiger counter.

Now, thanks to *The Dog I.Q. Test* (Penguin Books, $7.95), I know for sure Sophie isn't playing dumb. She's an honest-to-goodness dummy.

The Dog I.Q. Test consists of seventy questions that rate a dog's visual, audio, social and domestic skills.

Here's a sample question: Take a piece of scrap paper and crinkle it up into a ball in front of your dog. Now toss the paper to it. Your dog:

a) brings it back to you

b) begins to tear it into a hundred tiny bits with its teeth

c) watches it land on the floor, then just stares at it

d) swats at the paper with its paw or plays with it

e) is not interested in such a boring object.

Lassie, of course, would paste the pieces back together, correct the grammar (don't say "crinkle up," just "crinkle" is fine) and return it via Federal Express.

Sophie tried to eat the paper.

Before publishing, the authors tested hundreds of dogs from around the world, including a pedigree Lhasa apso named Toto from Houston.

Based on these results, the I.Q Test ranks dogs in seven groups, from "blissfully ignorant" (under seventy points) to "canine genius" (114 points and higher).

Sophie scored only sixty-eight points. Who doesn't want to be blissful?

The Dog I.Q. Test has a separate exam for dog owners. I expected to score big points here. After all, I always solve the puzzle on Wheel of Fortune before the contestants do.

I'm a terrific pet owner from way back. In high school, my wood-shop project was a dog bed.

Sample question from the book: What kind of sleeping arrangements have you provided for your dog?

a) It has its own dog bed

b) it has its own pillow or blanket

c) no special arrangements

d) it has free use of anywhere in the house.

I couldn't answer this one. Sophie not only sleeps in my bed, she has first dibs on all the good places. I twist and bend like a circus contortionist so I won't disturb her. If I accidentally bump her, she growls like a pit bull. I apologize for being so inconsiderate. And I never mention her snoring. Or her weight.

I cook a fresh hamburger for her dinner, which I mix with the most expensive dog food I can find.

I wonder, does Toto the Brain get hamburger for supper each night?

I love ice cream but I don't buy chocolate fudge ripple anymore because I read dogs shouldn't eat chocolate. Now I get cookies 'n' cream, which is her favorite, not mine.

What I can't figure out is, if Sophie's an idiot, and I'm so darn brilliant, how come she's got me trained so well?

Love Stinks

For Valentine's Day, here is a love story.

The most disgusting, smelliest love story you've ever heard.

It happened last Saturday night at the big Barbecue Cook-off in the Astrodome parking lot. Investor banker Kelly Covington and wife Kelly (yes, they have the same name) were in the middle of dinner when Mrs. Kelly, a sales rep at Channel 20 decided to use the Port-a-Potty.

If you remember, Saturday night was very chilly. She was wearing gloves.

Inside the Port-a-Potty, when she pulled off her left glove, her diamond wedding ring came flying off, too.

Like they say, "it" happens.

"My ring!" she screamed, and bolted from the Port-a-Potty like a bullrider coming out of Chute Five. The ring is a family heirloom. By the time she reached the dinner tent, tears were rolling down her cheeks and she was shaking uncontrollably.

"I thought my ring was gone forever, you know, halfway to China," she said.

"Then I realized that Port-a-Potties aren't like real toilets. They have a tank down there that holds everything until someone takes it away. My ring wasn't lost, it was just trapped in a very unpleasant place."

Husband Kelly saw his wife bawling and asked what happened. When she told him, he wondered, "What should we do?"

It was one of those questions where you already know the answer.

"You've got to go in there and get it back!" she cried.

This sounds like an episode of "I Love Lucy," if they still made "I Love Lucy" and showed it on late-night cable access. Turns out this Port-a-Potty mishap wasn't all that uncommon. Two nights earlier, another husband was called upon to retrieve a sunken diamond bracelet.

Husband Kelly found a pair of those heavy-duty rubber gloves that go up to your elbow. They use them at rodeo time for cooking massive amounts of barbecue and diving into icy barrels of beer.

"Then I wrapped a big Hefty garbage bag around my arm and went in. It was the single worst thing I've ever done," he said. "There I was, elbow deep, fishing around in a public toilet while my wife was holding a flashlight, crying her eyes out. Yeah, this was everything I thought married life would be."

He figures the tank holds about thirty gallons and it was half-filled. He dredged every ounce of it for twenty minutes and came up empty.

That's when wife Kelly leaned on the side wall of the Port-a-Potty and spotted the ring wedged in a crack in the floor. It never was down the toilet. She was elated, but now she had a new problem: How do you tell your husband he's been letting his fingers do the walking in a public toilet for twenty minutes for nothing?

Guess what, though? He was so happy to escape the toilet that he didn't mind. He didn't even yell or anything.

"It was a disgusting, retching experience. But I really don't think I did it for nothing. I was doing something for my wife," he said.

I told you it was a love story.

Check, Mate

LONDON—Garry Kasparov, the greatest chess player in history, was fidgety and cranky.

He was on the verge of defeating Nigel Short to retain his world's title. But the crowd was making it difficult for him to concentrate. Kasparov muttered to the judges and stomped off stage.

One judge held up a large sign that said "SILENCE." Then an announcement was made.

"We have an official complaint that the players can hear rustling of paper and loud breathing."

Loud breathing? Well, excuse us for living.

I went to game nineteen of the Professional Chess Association's championship match last week at the Savoy Theatre in London. I've seen livelier wax museums.

First, chess isn't like the Super Bowl, where they play one game and crown a champion. Football players run and sweat. Chess players sit for an hour and push a plastic horsey around a checkerboard. At one point, Short stared at the board for fifty-two minutes without making a move. I thought he died.

I grew nostalgic for the rock 'em, sock 'em excitement of a Weather Channel forecast.

Each chess game can take six hours. A chess match lasts twenty-four games played over three weeks. A win is worth one point. A draw (or tie) is worth a half-point. The first player to reach twelve and a half points wins.

Even though Kasparov clinched the title last week, the rules insist all twenty-four games be played. I smell a television contract.

This thing could still be going on.

Kasparov won $1.7 million. Nobody dumped Gatorade on him. He didn't receive a locker-room phone call from Prince Charles.

Short, who won only one game, took home $900,000.

Tickets originally were priced at $70. When nobody showed up, they lowered the tickets to $30. The Savoy Theatre holds only 1,000 people. My press badge said No. 766. I think the chess match lost money.

Although he never acknowledged the crowd (except to squeal on heavy breathers), Kasparov seemed like an interesting guy.

In 1985, he became the youngest world's champion ever at age twenty-two. A political activist, he lives in Moscow with his wife and daughter.

Short is from England, although he's no local favorite. He has pasty white skin, thick lips and thicker glasses. A British chess columnist called him a "dweeb."

Short looks like the kid in chemistry who wouldn't let you copy his homework. I'll bet anything he has a messy apartment with no TV. And there's cat hair everywhere.

All matches start at three p.m. sharp. Each player gets two hours to make forty moves. If, at the end of four hours, nobody's won, they get two more hours. At any time, one player can ask the other if he wants to call a draw. Most games end this way.

Sixteen of the first twenty-two games ended in a tie. In sports, they say that a tie is like kissing your sister. After a chess match, you and your sister would have to get married.

Everyone in the audience is given a headset to hear play-by-play and analysis from two Grandmasters in the balcony. Early on, one commentator said, "Short is employing the Sicilian defense, which is named after Harry Sicilian."

To chess fans, this was the funniest joke ever told. A shudder of laughter swept the Savoy. The worried commentator added, "Keep your titters down to a whisper."

Dweeb complained about the titters.
The next day, the commentator was fired.

Who's on First?

FINLAND—Drive north a few hours from this tiny village in Eastern Finland and you cross the Arctic Circle. Drive the same distance east and you're in Russia.

This is where they play *pesapallo*, the Finnish version of frostbitten baseball.

It may be the middle of nowhere, but it's pretty darn close to America's national pastime.

They play *pesapallo* because they love the sport. Their only financial reward is a free lunch and bus fare. No *pesapallo* player, not even the mighty Kari Kuusiniemi, the Babe Ruth of Finland, has ever charged for an autograph.

I went to my first *pesapallo* game Sunday afternoon. Siilinjarvi Pesis played Vaasan Maila in a do-or-die game for the home team.

As every sports fan knows, when Siilinjarvi plays Vaasan, you throw out the record books.

At first glance, *pesapallo* does look like baseball. The words even sound the same. Teams get three outs an inning. Both squads have nine players who do a lot of spitting. End of similarities.

In *pesapallo*, the *syottaja* (pitcher) stands next to the *lyoja* (batter) and flips a lime green ball straight up, hoping to land it on home base, a wooden disc the size and shape of a manhole cover.

The batter tries to hit it where they ain't, and sprints to first base, sixty feet down the left foul line.

Hey, you're going the wrong way!

Naturally, this ruins the old Abbott and Costello routine.

Who's on first?

The third baseman!

The runner's next goal is second base, ninety-five feet straight across the infield to the right foul line. Third base is 100 feet back the other way to a spot behind first base.

Each team has one "joker," the Finnish designated hitter, who wears a psychedelic jockey's jersey and bats each inning whenever his coach feels the whim.

If I sound mixed up, it's because I sat next to Jouni Mutanen, the mayor of Siilinjarvi, and he explained the rules. You'd think I'd be used to a mayor who mumbles by now.

Up to this year, *pesapallo* games lasted nine innings. Now there's a new rule: Games are divided into two halves, each lasting four innings. If one team wins both halves, everybody goes home to take a sauna. If the teams split halves, they go into extra innings.

Finland does not have professional athletics. For example, distance runner Lasse Viren won three gold medals in the 1972 and 1976 Olympics. Today he is a policeman.

Pesapallo players don't do commercials, not even for Hart Sport Drink, the Finnish answer to Gatorade.

They don't play the Finnish national anthem before *pesapallo* games Sunday, the teams warmed up to Eric Clapton's Greatest Hits.

There was joy in Siilinjarvi as the home team won the first half 4-2 on Juha Niiranen's *kunnari* (home run) in the bottom of the fourth, then swept the second half, 2-0.

Niiranen was named "Player of the Game" and received a gift box of plastic dishes. Niiranen is a student at the University of Kuopio. He heard about the baseball strike in America and wouldn't mind being a millionaire *pesapallo* player himself.

"Of course, I don't think that is possible. Not in Finland. Not for many years," he shrugged.

Let Barry Bonds have his $43 million contract. Niiranen has something considerably more practical: a place setting for eight.

A Phone Addict?

My first phone call of the day comes at six a.m. from friends who host a morning radio show in New York. The last call comes at about eleven p.m. from someone who can't get it through his head that it's way past bedtime.

In between, I spend most of my day on the phone. I'm a phone addict. If I go outside to shoot baskets, I take a portable phone with me. If I take a bath, I take a phone into the bathroom. I've dropped a couple in the tub.

I thought I was pretty hot stuff on the phone—until I heard about the crazy lady they just arrested in Japan.

I read about her in one of those screwy British tabloids I get at the out-of-town newspaper stand.

"A Japanese woman has been arrested for making 150,000 nuisance phone calls to a housewife whose happiness she envied. Takato Sato of Shizoula, near Tokyo, averaged fifty calls a day over eight years. Police were only alerted when the victim had a nervous breakdown."

Now, I'm thinking, the victim was a housewife, right? That means she has a husband. Didn't he ever say, "Honey, that's the 100,000th crank call we've gotten. Think maybe we should get our number changed?"

And what about Takato, the woman who let her fingers do all the walking? Talk about toiling in anonymity.

I have another friend who calls me every day at five p.m., in the heart of my napping time.

"The red light on my phone was blinking, so I knew you were sleeping," he says.

He thinks this is funny. Then I can't get back to sleep and my whole day is ruined.

I'm not sure I buy Takato's excuse, though. So she was envious of the other person?

I'm envious of any tennis player who makes $5 million a year but can't find two socks that match.

But I don't call Andre Agassi fifty times a day.

Another thing about phones. I hate voice mail. I hate leaving messages. I say something dumb, and there's no way to take it back.

I talked to someone who works at the phone company. He said that in Japan, you get charged for each call you make. Can you imagine Takato's phone bill? No wonder she's single and the other woman found a husband.

Sometimes my nap is interrupted by a recorded phone call.

"Congratulations, you have been chosen at random to receive a free Florida vacation. To claim your prize you must ..."

I've never stayed on long enough to hear what I have to do. I'm sure they want me to buy property near a lake somewhere.

How about when you dial the phone, it starts ringing, and you've completely forgotten who you're calling? That happens to me at least twice a day. You pray you recognize the "hello."

I have people who call me and assume I recognize their voice.

"Hi, how are you doing?"

I'm OK.

"What's going on?"

Nothing, I'm just sitting here.

"Anything new happening?"

I feel like screaming: "Give me a clue here. I can't make small talk forever. Who the heck is this?"

What about the woman in Japan who had the nervous breakdown? Was it a gradual thing? Was she fine for the first 149,000 calls and then went bonkers without warning?

Couldn't her husband see this coming?

But what if Takato isn't as loony as this story makes her out to be?

What if Takato made the calls, they talked, and then Takato realized she forgot to tell her something? So she called right back. I've done that myself.

OK, maybe not 150,000 times.

Match Point!

Bjorn Borg won six French Opens and five Wimbledon championships. He's made millions as one of the world's all-time greatest tennis players.

My crowning achievement in tennis was in 1992 and 1993 when I won the Fondren Tennis Club championship. I won a trophy the first year. The next year I asked for a pair of socks instead.

Thursday afternoon, I lived a tennis hacker's fantasy.

I played Bjorn Borg on center court at the River Oaks Country Club. He was preparing for next week's Sixty-first River Oaks Invitational.

The deal was, Borg had to play hard. I wanted to look across the net, see a legend, and get my butt beat something awful.

Borg had no problem with that.

Borg looked pretty much like he did back in the late '70s when he won his five Wimbledons. His long hair was tied back and stuffed under a baseball cap. He needed a shave. His fingers were taped. He wore Tretorn sneakers.

We warmed up for about five minutes. Borg floated one to my backhand, which I returned, doing my best Borg two-handed imitation.

"You hit with two hands like me," he noticed.

How observant. I learned how to play tennis by watching him beat Jimmy Connors and John McEnroe on television.

He spun his racket to see who'd serve first. I called "up" and it came up "up."

"You serve," I said. I read Brad Gilbert's book, *Winning Ugly*, and he says you should always receive first. Gilbert coaches Andre Agassi so he must know what he's talking about.

Borg served wide to my forehand. I blocked it back. Borg smacked it to my forehand again and rushed the net. I hit a passing shot up the line.

A clean winner.

Forget the Fondren Tennis Club trophy and the pair of socks. I just won a point from Bjorn Borg!

I did not win another point in our one-set match. To say he beat me like a drum would be an understatement. This was the drum solo from "In-A-Gadda-Da-Vida."

I knew my chances were slim. We played on clay, Borg's specialty. He won six French Opens on clay. I once made an ashtray out of clay at camp.

This was the worst I've ever been beaten in anything. Borg won twenty-four straight points. The set was over in ten minutes. I was huffing and puffing, trying to track down his shots. He didn't miss.

He hit one lob that cleared my racket by an inch and landed inside the baseline by an inch. I found myself watching him glide around the court. I hit my best drop shot. He reached it in a flash and hit an even better drop shot for a winner.

My only chance to win a point was for him to double fault. He didn't.

Most of the points ended with me hitting the ball wide. The rest of the balls I hit long or into the net.

Borg did not ace me. He spun his serve in, except for a couple of scorchers that nearly twisted the racket out of my hand.

At match point, when I had lost twenty-three in a row, a friend yelled out, "I don't think you're going to win."

One volley later, I was shaking Borg's hand over the net and congratulating him. Just like John McEnroe and Jimmy Connors used to. And those guys never won the Fondren Tennis Club title. 🎾

Flowers or Frisbees Only

Now I know how a baseball player feels when he takes batting practice but never gets to hit.

I wanted to throw dishes in a Greek restaurant, like in the movie *Zorba the Greek*. Done with my salad: *Crash!* Soup finished: *Splat!* The lamb kebabs were delicious: *Kaboom!*

I wanted to heave a ninety-five-mph dinner plate like Oddjob trying to decapitate James Bond. I figured it'd be a snap. I practically majored in Frisbee in college.

I went to a restaurant called Athens At Night in the old section of town. It advertised authentic Greek food, music and dancing. I could hear the dishes crashing already.

That's when I got the news: Greeks don't throw dishes.

Not any more.

"We have had a law for maybe five years, you cannot throw the dishes," said tour guide George Mandicos. "The singers and musicians were getting hurt. So it was made a rule you cannot do this. You can still find a small restaurant maybe that will let you, but it will be in a bad section, too dangerous for tourists."

Breaking dishes, it turns out, wasn't exactly an ancient Greek custom. It started one drunken night about fifty or sixty years ago.

"A rich man was very unhappy and sad. He was eating dinner in a restaurant and thinking about his problems," Mandicos said. "He was having many drinks and he began to get drunk. The more he got drunk the happier he got. Suddenly he stood up and threw, not just the dishes, but the whole table at the singers. He yelled out, 'Tonight I am paying for everything!' The other people threw their dishes and everybody went crazy. When we Greeks have a party we really raise hell.

"That is how the custom began. The thing that made it popular to everybody around the world was the movie *Zorba the Greek*. After that, people who came to a Greek restaurant expected to throw their dishes. The dancers complained because the dishes were cutting the bottoms of their feet."

The bottom line, not feet, is what really stopped the custom.

"You break one dish, it costs a dollar. But when you break a thousand dishes each night, it was very expensive," Mandicos said.

"In other countries, you can find Greek restaurants where they throw dishes. But in Greece, we now ask you to throw flowers. The dancers like it much more."

I considered suggesting paper plates or Chinet. But why meddle?

The Athens At Night restaurant was packed with 300 tourists, mostly from Italy and Turkey. Two or three of them weren't chain-smoking directly on my food.

The master of ceremonies looked like Eddie Fisher making his fifteenth comeback, this time opening for Buddy Hackett on a cruise ship. It was like getting dressed up for the wedding of a cousin you can't stand. You know it will be a lousy time, but you'll have some laughs on the way home.

The first song was "Never On Sunday" It was also the last song, and a couple songs in between.

The dancers jumped and twisted so high I thought they were going to shout, "I'm going to Disney World" at the end.

During the *Zorba The Greek* medley, I got swept up in a conga line that snaked its way into the street. It was the first time I danced in public since I judged the 1990 Halloween costume party at Wish's couples-only club. I'm still apologizing for that one.

After each song, the Athens At Night crowd yelled, "*Opa!,*" which means, I later found out, "Hip, hip, hooray" in Greek.

I didn't know *"Opa!"* and thought they were screaming "Oprah!"—so I ordered a triple helping of baklava.

I may have broken my diet, but I didn't even chip a plate. 🎆

Nobody Whistled

My favorite movie of all time is *The Bridge on the River Kwai*. I love watching the British prisoners of war build that bridge, while their Japanese captors scratch their heads in grudging admiration. The movie won seven Academy Awards, including best picture, in 1958.

During my vacation in Thailand, I jumped at the chance to visit Kanchanaburi Province (about three hours west of Bangkok) and see the real-life Bridge on the River Kwai.

Actually, I was surprised to learn the bridge is still there. Wasn't it blown to bits, right as the first Japanese train was crossing it, at the end of the movie? I honestly thought the movie was a true story.

I was surprised to learn that almost everything about *The Bridge on the River Kwai* was different from what really happened near the Thailand-Burma border during World War II.

A bridge, actually two bridges, were built by prisoners of war over the Khwae Yai River between 1942 and 1943. The first was made of wood, the second of steel.

The name of the river is pronounced "kwah"—like the word "quack" without the c and k.

The bridges were a key part of the Death Railway through Japanese-occupied Thailand and Burma (Myanmar, today). The Japanese needed the railway to transport soldiers and weapons to the India border, from which they attacked British military positions in India.

The movie is a nice story, about enemies cooperating during war, with sort of a happy ending (from our point of view, anyway).

In the movie, the prisoners were treated kindly. It seems the

Japanese commander liked the British soldiers more than his own troops.

In real life, the prisoners did not happily whistle the Colonel Bogey March while they worked. This was a death labor camp. Thousands of prisoners, not just from England, but also from the United States, Australia, Thailand and Holland, died building the bridges.

A hundred thousand more "volunteer" laborers from Burma, Malaysia and Indonesia died, too. They perished of malnutrition, starvation, malaria, cruel beatings and sheer exhaustion.

The bridges were completed in April 1943 and continued in operation for twenty months until American bombers destroyed them.

The steel bridge was rebuilt after the war. It still stands, and it still carries trains over the river.

Today, the area is dotted with resort hotels and restaurants. Where soldiers were worked to death, now tour buses pause for photos. Tourists in *Bridge on the River Kwai* T-shirts walk across the bridge, whistling like in the movie.

Two cemeteries and the JEATH Museum honor the prisoners in Kanchanaburi. The museum's name comes from the primary countries involved in the bridges' construction: Japan, England, America, Thailand and Holland.

The museum is a replica of the bamboo huts that housed the prisoners. The walls are lined with gruesome photos and mementos of the camp.

Visitors see prisoners wearing loincloths that barely hang on their emaciated bodies. They see straw-covered benches, with each prisoner allowed thirty inches of space on which to sleep. Every meal was the same, rice with salt. The prisoners had no soap, no medical supplies, no chance of escape and little hope of surviving.

When a prisoner violated his captors' law, he would be sentenced to "the hole," an underground tomb, where temperatures climbed to 130 degrees. Some prisoners spent thirty months in the hole, never seeing sunlight.

After visiting the real bridge, the JEATH Museum and the prisoner cemeteries, I went home and watched *The Bridge on the River Kwai* again. It's still my favorite movie.

Only now I see a sad ending.

Fries *con Nada*

This week I reached out for a super-size order of McDonald's french fries with a two-ounce portion of McDonald's new cheese sauce.

Total calories: 661. Fat grams: 35.

You've got to hand it to McDonald's. Despite statistics showing that thirty-five percent of American adults are dangerously tubby, McDonald's has introduced a greasy, fat-laden cheese sauce to top its greasy, fat-laden french fries.

Thanks a bunch. Frankly, I was concerned I wasn't getting enough fat in my french fries.

How about if I order a bacon double cheeseburger, too, and wash it down with a refreshing bottle of Wesson? And while you're at it, just inject a couple pounds of Crisco directly into my veins for dessert.

McDonald's dipping sauce, which looks and tastes suspiciously like microwaved Cheez Whiz, costs twenty-five cents. (In McDonaldspeak, microwaving is called "q-ing.")

This is the first time McDonald's has charged extra for what is essentially a condiment.

And it's one more attempt to drag the noble french fry through the mud. Cheese on top of french fries is the most shocking coverup since Watergate. Only worse. Watergate only threatened to bring down our democracy. McDonald's cheese sauce is messing up my lunch!

French fries don't need cheese. They don't need beer batter. They don't need seasoned coating. They don't need nothin'.

Our friends in Europe have completely lost their minds when they pour mayonnaise on their fries. It's like they sat down and said,

"What's even worse for you than cheese? Oh yeah, mayonnaise!"

French fries are fine by themselves. Give me a steaming, grease-stained paper bag full of fries, salted and peppered to death, with ketchup on the side. Then leave me alone. Don't ask for just one or two. If you want french fries, I'll buy you a whole bag for yourself. I'm not selfish, I'm just hungry.

French fries are my favorite part of the traditional burger-fries-Coke fast-food meal.

I don't care where you go, you can make a better burger at home. Cokes taste better from a bottle, too.

Hamburger restaurants do french fries best. At least, McDonald's does.

You know, I could almost understand Burger King or Wendy's slopping cheese on their fries. Their fries are pretty run-of-the-mill.

McDonald's has the best fries, plain and simple. And that's how they should be eaten.

Grade-A All the Way

The first time Jill McNett called me, I thought it was a put-on.

She had read my review of a Neil Diamond concert at Compaq Center. Now she wanted to take me out to dinner. "Come on, we'll talk about Neil Diamond," she said in a soft British accent. "Plus I have a surprise."

I had no idea what I was getting myself into.

We met at Rao's restaurant on Richmond. McNett found out that's where Diamond had eaten the night before. She arranged for executive chef Tony Rao to prepare the identical meal that Diamond had.

We ate fried calamari, involtini di pollo (chicken breast stuffed with sausage and spinach) and angel hair pasta with tomato cream sauce and lump crab meat. Chef Rao prepared it exactly as he did for Diamond, down to the last lump.

For two hours that night, Jill, her husband, Jim, and I talked about Diamond. Not for a single moment did the conversation get off Diamond.

Actually, Jill did all the talking. Jim and I just listened.

She talked about his music, his love life, his movie career, his concerts. His homes. His cars. His interview with Barbara Walters. His hair. His eyebrows.

Before that dinner, I thought I was a pretty good Diamond fan. At least I used to be—for his rock 'n' roll oldies, like "Thank the Lord for Nighttime."

Back in the '70s, I was working at a record store in New Jersey when Diamond booked himself in the Winter Garden Theater on Broadway for twenty concerts. The Columbia record rep gave us free tickets. The other guys working in the store were too cool for Diamond, so I wound up going to sixteen concerts that month.

Still, I wasn't in the same league as Jill McNett. She breathed Neil Diamond.

That was an unforgettable dinner in 1992, and the start of an even more unforgettable friendship with Jill.

I had never met anybody who was that big a fan of anything. I mean, I like Paul McCartney, but I'm not going to an expensive restaurant and ordering one of Linda's veggie burgers to go.

Jill felt joy in Diamond's music. She was battling multiple sclerosis and played his albums during her physical therapy. She said his music took her pain away. Whenever Diamond came to town, she'd roll her wheelchair as close to the stage as possible.

I wrote a few paragraphs in the paper about this "Grade-A bonkers Neil Diamond fan" who took me out to a Neil Diamond dinner. Every time after that, whenever she called, she'd giggle, "This is the Grade-A bonkers Neil Diamond fan."

If she heard a rumor that Diamond was coming to town, she'd call and ask me to track it down. A couple of years ago, Diamond played Fort Worth but passed on Houston. She blew a fuse over that.

Every couple of years after that, we'd go out to dinner. I insisted that we eat normal food, no more celebrity chow-downs. She came to my wedding. She gave me a portable cassette player so I could "listen to my Neil Diamond on the tennis court." I didn't even try to explain that my opponent might not enjoy that.

Years before I met Jill, I wrote a story about Diamond that wound up in his concert program. In return, Diamond autographed a bunch of photos for me.

I had one of the photos framed and gave it to Jill. As Grade-A bonkers as she was, she had never met Diamond. Still, I had to practically force her to take it.

Jill's health deteriorated over the years. Her voice got a little weaker, she had trouble hearing. I'd always ask, "How are you feeling?" More and more often, the answer was, "Not so good." Then we'd launch into a one-way debate on how come Diamond's new album is all ballads.

Jill was so forgiving of him. When Diamond was rumored to have left his wife for a twenty-one-year-old rodeo queen, Jill figured it was "just a phase." She was more worried that he might put out a country album.

Jill died last week at age fifty-one. For the seven years I knew her, all we ever talked about was Diamond. Then I read her obituary.

I never knew that she once won "Student of the Year" honors at the Park Lance College of Further Education in Leeds, England.

I didn't know that she spoke Dutch, German and French fluently. I didn't know that she once lived in Libya or that she was a gourmet cook or that she was a relentless fund-raiser for local schools. I didn't even know that she and Jim were married for thirty years.

I only knew that she was a Grade-A bonkers Neil Diamond fan. I'm not surprised that she was Grade-A everything else, too.

It wasn't Cappucino

Aphrodite, the mythological goddess of love and beauty, was born in this resort town on the western tip of Cyprus.

Thousands of years later, the myth lives on. Only now, Aphrodite is the goddess of neon signs and tacky souvenirs. Walk downtown and you'll pass vendors selling Aphrodite thermometers, plaster statues of Aphrodite with a clock in her stomach, T-shirts, pens, pencils, candy bars and loud, awful neckties that glow in the dark.

If you don't want to walk, call the Aphrodite Taxi Co. Better yet, stay at the downtown Aphrodite Hotel. Hungry? The Aphrodite Rooftop Restaurant makes terrific kebabs.

(Not everything in Paphos is named for the goddess of love. Teen-agers have to eat somewhere, too. Down the road, you'll find Wimpy's Burgers and Fat Mama's pizza parlor.)

Tourists can visit the Baths of Aphrodite (don't drink the water) and even her birthplace, the jutting rock known as Petra tou Romiou, just a few yards off shore in south Paphos.

According to tradition, if a woman takes a midnight dip in the baths of Aphrodite, she will regain her virginity. Another version says the woman simply will become more beautiful.

Local taverns pour Aphrodite Wine. If a man drinks enough, it will make a woman more beautiful, too. Especially around closing time.

There is a shrine to Aphrodite, where women take home a pebble to guarantee their husbands or boyfriends will stay faithful.

Take a sip from the Fontana Amorosa, near the baths, and you'll fall in love with the next thing that moves.

The local soccer team isn't called the Aphrodites. That wouldn't sound threatening enough. So they did the next best thing. They're named the Adonises, after Aphrodite's lover.

Let's say one of her lovers. They didn't call Aphrodite the goddess of love for nothing. Compared to Aphrodite, Heidi Fleiss is a one-man woman. Aphrodite, whose name in Roman mythology is Venus, liked to spread her loving around. She had at least six children and a dozen different lovers. It didn't matter if her sex partners were gods or mere mortals. Or men, for that matter. Among the notches on her bedpost: Hephaestus, Ares, Hermes, Dionysus, Poseidon, Anchises and Adonis.

An impressive array, but she still trails Elizabeth Taylor by one husband.

It's too bad Aphrodite was born thousands of years ago. She'd be a perfect guest on the Sally Jessy Raphael show. She'd push Tonya and Nancy and Michael Jackson off the National Enquirer's front page. Madonna would call her for sex tips.

Just consider the way Aphrodite was born. One day, Cronos the Titan got so angry at his rotten father Uranus that he castrated pop.

There goes Lorena Bobbitt off the Enquirer's front page too.

Uranus' genitals fell into the sea and floated for a long time. A white foam collected around them. The foam was fertilized and up sprang Aphrodite. She hopped aboard a giant seashell and surfed into Paphos.

That's how she got her name. *Aphro* means foam in Greek. It wasn't because she combed her hair like Linc on *The Mod Squad*. *Dite* is someone who dives into water.

Right from the start, she was a knockout. Everywhere she stepped in Paphos, colorful flowers bloomed.

Zeus, king of the gods, took an immediate liking to Aphrodite and made her the goddess of beauty, love, joy, laughter and fertility. The way some tell it, Zeus took more than just a liking, but save that for tomorrow's Sally Jessy show.

Like most beautiful goddesses, Aphrodite was plenty of trouble.

Other women were so jealous they did nutty things, like the time Helen of Troy ditched her schnook of a husband and chased her boyfriend, Paris, to Troy because she thought Paris was messing around with Aphrodite. That touched off the Trojan War, that's all.

Aphrodite had other responsibilities besides just looking like the cover of *Cosmo* magazine. She protected women who had dangerous jobs, especially prostitutes. Hookers were allowed to ply their trade in her temples. Festivals in honor of Aphrodite usually wound up like swingers' parties. When girls turned sixteen, they'd come to Aphrodite's bath house and wait for a man to take their virginity.

Aphrodite had different last names in different cities in ancient Greece. In her hometown, her name was Aphrodite Paphia. In another city, she was Aphrodite Philomeis, because of her love of laughter.

In one town, she was known as Aphrodite Calipyge because of the delicate roundness of her tush. *Calipyge* is an ancient Greek Cypriot word for nice rear end.

If you don't believe it, check out the anatomically correct Aphrodite cigarette lighters, available at corner souvenir shops.

We'll Drive, *Señor*

Nuevo Laredo, right across the border in Mexico, is a trip. It's like Saturday night, seven days a week. The food is great, especially on *domingo* (Sunday), when the Marco Pollo restaurant offers one-and-a-half chickens for the price of one.

The streets are jammed with tourists buying everything under the sun they don't need. I once bought a sombrero big enough to take a bath in. They have a guy down there who, for $2, will write your name on a grain of rice. He doesn't use a nuclear microscope or steroided-out jumbo rice, either.

He just sticks a pinky in his mouth, dips out one grain and prints your name on it with a plain Bic pen. His handwriting is perfect. He evens draws a rose or a heart on the other side. Then he puts the rice in a little tube and you wear it around your neck like a piece of junk jewelry from the Home Shopping Channel.

I'm thinking about adopting this guy and bringing him to Houston. I'll make a fortune off him at Mexican restaurants. Except from now on, the price goes up to $3.

My only problem with Nuevo Laredo is it's five hours away, a straight, boring shot down Highway 59. Between the lousy scenery, the gas, the wear and tear on your car and the horrible fritzy radio stations on the way, it's a long trip.

Then I found out about a deal Greyhound is running. Round-trip bus fare is only $52. That's practically break-even gas money. But if you buy your ticket three days in advance, you get one ticket free.

The second ticket, the free one, that's mine. The first ticket is yours.

My Mexico-traveling buddy Reg "Third Degree" Burns and I

bought tickets for the 3:30 a.m. Saturday night bus. We thought who in their right mind will be taking a bus to Mexico that late at night in the middle of the weekend?

The bus was packed. Not one seat empty.

You haven't lived until you've hung out at the downtown bus station at three in the morning. They have a twenty-four-hour Kentucky Fried Chicken store inside the terminal. I'd never seen a vending machine that dispenses whole pints of ice cream. This wasn't exactly a health food crowd. I fit right in.

Once everybody got seated on the bus, which took longer than it should have, the driver laid down the law. No smoking. No loud music. No yelling. No taking off your shoes because your feet might stink. I'm not sure if he was kidding about the shoes thing, but I'm wholeheartedly in favor of the rule.

They enforce the rules, too. The driver said if anybody lights up a Marlboro, he'll stop the bus and personally put out your butt. He'll put out your cigarette, too.

The seats are very skinny. I'm a normal-size guy, and I was hanging one cheek off. I scrunched a sweater against the window, jammed my head in there and went beddy-bye. I woke up for the pit stop in San Antonio, reloaded my doughnut stash and continued dozing to Laredo.

The bus was clean. The air conditioning was on. The toilet worked. It's the only way to go.

The Greyhound station in Laredo is about five blocks from the border bridge. The fee to cross into Mexico is thirty-five cents. Expect to wait a few minutes behind a conga line of tourists trying to fish thirty-five lint-coated pennies from the bottom of their purses.

Just across the border, you'll be met by a group of helpful young men. They'll show you how to buy bullfight tickets, diet pills, dinner, jewelry, discos, romance and the finest eye and dental care non-reimbursable by American insurance.

Leave yourself an extra ten minutes getting back across the border. Sometimes the guard will ask to see what's in your shopping bag. And then maybe a drug-sniffing dog will take a good whiff of you.

The bus leaves right on the dot. Whether the dog found you aromatically pleasing or not.

Get a Grip

No more wrestling for me. At least not until I heal up from Saturday night.

I was the guest referee for a big Dog Collar Match between Mad Dog and War Dog at the Humble Bingo Hall. These two guys used to be tag-team partners. Now they hate each other's guts.

It seems Mad Dog snuck around and messed with War Dog's girlfriend (possibly a true story).

I took the referee job because I have a bad habit of saying yes to almost anything, as long as it's far off in the future. When someone calls and asks if I'd judge a cow-chip-tossing contest, I ask when it'll be. If they say it's not until next July, I say yes.

Next thing I know, it's July and I'm ducking a hunk of flying cow doody Next month I'm judging a chicken-soup contest and a hot-dog art fair. I'm going to model sportswear in the spring. I'm already signed up to be the commencement speaker at a Houston high school next year.

That's how I got to the Humble Bingo Hall. They asked me a long time ago.

By the way, nice place, the Humble Bingo Hall.

Since everybody over six months old knows wrestling is ninety-nine percent show business, I won't be giving away any secrets here. But before the match, we went over the "script".

Mad Dog was going to win the match by dragging War Dog around the ring and touching all four corners. Then War Dog's manager, "A.C.," would start yelling at me for being a lousy referee.

At that point, War Dog would tiptoe behind me. A.C. would push me over, and I'd pretend to be hurt. I'd lie there "unconscious" for a minute until the other referee came to my rescue.

OK, it's not the height of sophisticated comedy, but we were in a hall where the night before people had been yelling, "B-7, N-34, O-54" and eating cold hot dogs.

The match went just as they said it would. Mad Dog won, and I raised his hand. That was where A.C. and War Dog decided to throw out the script and do some improvisational theater. They think they're Robin Williams, and I'm about to get hurt.

A.C. grabbed me by the shirt. I mean, he really grabbed me. He began questioning my parents' faithfulness to each other. Worse, he ripped my shirt. It was one of my favorite Bugle Boys.

War Dog kicked the back of my legs, and I tumbled to the mat. He jumped into the air and crashed his elbow into my chest.

Let me describe War Dog: He weighs 300 pounds. He went to a dentist and had his teeth permanently filed into fangs. He paints his fingernails black He wears bright red lipstick and Tammy Faye mascara. He's completely out of what's left of his mind.

When War Dog fell from the sky and bashed me, two thoughts popped into my brain:.

(1) I will never carry my car keys in my back pocket again.

(2) I wonder if Ben Taub Hospital rooms have cable TV?

Feeling frisky, War Dog cracked me with another elbow. I couldn't breathe. Then he started choking me and screaming, "I'll kill you!".

I just know this is going to wind up on Court TV.

And where was the other referee? I peeked out of the corner of my eye and saw him at the snack bar. How long does it take to cook a cold hot dog?

The heck with him. I got up, staggered out the front door and drove off .

His Ego's in Jeopardy

Thursday was "Annual Humiliation Day" for me—the *Jeopardy* tryouts.

This year was worse than ever. How am I supposed to know what condiment is named after the Hindustani word for "spice"? I guessed A-1 steak sauce.

Jeopardy tryouts were held, by invitation only, at the J. W. Marriott hotel on Westheimer.

"We had room for only 300 people so we asked viewers to send in postcards," said Channel 11 publicist Barbara Jordan. "We received 10,000 cards. The response to our *Jeopardy* auditions is always tremendous."

The test was *Jeopardy's* standard fifty-question humbler. Only stumpers on the $800 and $1,000 level were asked.

Geography: What is the largest of the Alpine lakes on the border of France and Switzerland?

Architecture: Who designed the Chelsea Hospital in 1661?

Edwin Walker from LaPorte sat in the row in front of me. Edwin's a pretty smart guy. He recently graduated from the University of Houston Law School. He's taking the bar exam this summer.

Edwin flunked the *Jeopardy* test as bad as I did.

"I didn't like the categories. There was too much literature—Russian literature," he said. "If the bar exam is this tough, I'm in big trouble."

Trying out for *Jeopardy* isn't like watching the game show on TV. That's where I shine. I win thousands—millions—on TV. I shout out answers like a computer with fresh batteries.

Plants: What is the source for linen and linseed oil?

I wrote down Kmart. That's where I get them.

Philosophy: Who was known as the Danish Socrates?

The only person I know from Denmark is Victor Borge.

I tossed in my pencil at Question number ten, which had something to do with a U.S. expatriate poetess who wrote a libretto for Virgil Thomson.

Where were categories like "TV Sitcoms" or "Tennis Players Who Grunt" or "Alvin Van Black's favorite desserts"?

The worst part is, they never did give us the correct answers. Seventy people took the *Jeopardy* audition in my group. Only eleven passed the test (thirty-five right answers) and were asked to play a mock game, "buzzing in" with a school bell.

That eliminated five more people. The final six went through a "personality evaluation."

Yes, personality does count in *Jeopardy*. They don't expect you to squeal like on *The Price Is Right*, but they don't want Lurch from *The Addams Family*, either.

The final six will be contacted during the next few months. They'll have to fly to Los Angeles at their own expense.

"Bring five different tops, no whites, no wild prints, just in case you keep winning," they were told.

I got this information secondhand. Claudia Perry, the *Post's* pop music critic, was one of the finalists. Claudia knew that Sally Field won the Oscar in 1984 for *Places In The Heart*. And she knew that Delaware was the first state to ratify the U.S. Constitution.

Claudia is probably going to win $50,000 plus a year's supply of Rice-a-Roni on *Jeopardy*.

I'm not jealous. I'll bet five dollars I can beat her at *American Gladiators*.

Making Whoopees!

TAIPEI, TAIWAN—Since the beginning of time, there has been but one guaranteed laugh.

The Whoopee Cushion.

You blow up a pink rubber bag, slip it under a seat cushion, and when somebody (preferably your teacher) sits down...Pfffft!

Hysterical!

In Taiwan, the island that gave us joy buzzers, the dribble glass, the fly in the ice cube trick, soap that turns your hands black, itching powder, squirting flowers and fake bloody thumbs, the Whoopee Cushion remains the all-time gag gift.

It was at 11 Allen 61, Lane 2, Section 8, in not a particularly scenic part of Taipei, that I met Fu-Yuan Shih.

If they ever build a Comedy Hall of Fame, well, forget inducting Fu-Yuan. They should name the place after him. Forty years ago, he invented the Whoopee Cushion. He is the Thomas Edison of belly laughs.

"My factory made rubber belts that children used to tie around their school books. You had one maybe? They were very popular," Fu-Yuan said. "During the process to make them, I tried to think of other uses for rubber. That is how I invented the Whoopee Cushion."

For the record, the first victim to unsuspectingly sit on a Whoopee Cushion was Fu-Yuan's good friend and business associate, Chen-Mu Chen. He's probably still laughing.

Fu-Yuan employs 130 people in his Whoopee Cushion factory. They mix the imported natural rubber, stretch it, dry it on the floor, slice the patterns and glue them together. Every step is done by hand.

Outside the factory, crates of finished Whoopee Cushions wait to be picked up. Fu-Yuan sends them to every "developed nation" in the world, he said. He does not sell them in Taiwan, however.

"Taiwanese are too conservative to find them funny," he said.

It costs twenty cents to produce one Whoopee Cushion. Fu-Yuan's profit on each cushion is only four cents.

But he sells a lot of them.

Get ready for this. Last year, he sold 800,000 dozen Whoopee Cushions!

"I knew they would be a good seller, but I am surprised by their long-term success," he said.

Whoopee Cushions have not changed in forty years. They still have the same artwork, the drawing of a woman screaming. The cushions still carry the warning, "Do not inflate too heavily."

Fu-Yuan said the demand increases each year. After all this time, he still laughs at his own joke. "If it wasn't funny, why am I selling so many of them?"

Business is so good that he will open a second factory late this summer. The new plant will be in mainland China, where labor costs are cheaper than in Taiwan.

That should help because summer is Fu-Yuan's busiest time of year. He's got Christmas Whoopee Cushion orders to fill.

His office is upstairs from the factory. It's a cluttered mess. Towering stacks of Whoopee Cushions cover his desk.

Fu-Yuan has four daughters and one son. All five children graduated college, tuition paid in full by Whoopee Cushions.

Daughter Debby graduated from the University of Florida with a degree in finance. She is the family accountant.

"One time at college, we were watching *The Cosby Show* and Bill Cosby used a Whoopee Cushion," Debby said. "I told my friends, 'My father invented that.' Nobody believed me."

Fu-Yuan recently expanded his product line to include jumping frogs, false mustaches and a whistle that sounds like you're blowing your nose. But the Whoopee Cushion will always be his pride and joy.

"Somebody else invented these other things," he said. "The Whoopee Cushion is mine."

3.

"Which Way to the Flea Market?"

Mad Dash
Through Europe

In Berlin, there's a bar called Klo—that's German slang for bathroom. Customers drink beer from a bedpan. They play sound effects of flushing toilets over the loudspeaker.

I've got to see this place!

The world's skinniest house, four stories high, only seven feet wide, is in Amsterdam.

I'll drop by.

I've got the address of the house where Zsa Zsa Gabor grew up in Budapest. Zsa Zsa says her cousin will pick me up at the train station and show me around the neighborhood.

During Oktoberfest in Munich, they have amusement park rides that are so dangerous they're not allowed in America. I'm going to ride the loop-de-loop until something awful happens.

This week, I'm traveling through Europe on a thrill ride that makes Oktoberfest look tame.

Ten cities in ten days. Ten nights on a train. No hotels.

I'm with Reg Burns, who works as an accountant but is better known for winning all-you-can-eat contests, and Oreste (Rusty) San Juan, who picks the ponies in The Post Sports section. In fact, Rusty paid for his trip with winnings from the quarter horse meet at Sam Houston Race Park.

Beavis and Butt-head in Europe.

We're going to do this trip as inexpensively as possible. I'm practicing how to order hamburgers in French, Dutch, Danish, Polish and German. I'm hooked on McPhonics.

We waited until fall because that's when airline tickets to Europe drop below $600. Then we got Eurail train tickets. For $498, you can go anywhere you want for fifteen days in first class.

If we paid for each train trip, it would cost more than $1,000. With the money I'm saving, maybe I won't have to eat McDonald's every meal.

Overnight sleeping compartments on the train are $24. That's a lot less than a hotel, plus you don't blow a whole day getting to the next city.

Granted, sleeping on a train isn't the Ritz-Carlton. You get a pillow, a sheet, a blanket and five strange bunkmates who most likely snore.

If they're young, your bunkmates will think they can sing, too.

Our European strategy is simple. Take the morning tour bus in each city. Visit one unusual attraction in the afternoon. Have dinner. Get back on the train. Wake up in a new city.

Repeat daily.

Day One is Paris. Then it's on to Amsterdam, Copenhagen, Berlin, Warsaw, Budapest, Prague, Munich, Monte Carlo and Hamburg.

I've contacted travel experts to help me find a weird or unusual tourist trap in each city.

No Eiffel Tower for us in Paris. I wanted to see why no one's going to Euro Disney.

Did you know the world's biggest flea market is in Warsaw?

The only serious museum devoted to eroticism is in Copenhagen?

We're traveling light. All I've taken is one small suitcase, two pairs of jeans, a couple of sweaters and my oldest, most worn-out socks and underwear. I'm tossing the socks and underwear each morning.

I've got a bright yellow rain suit. I tried it on in the store. I look like the Gorton's fisherman.

I'm also bringing a portable computer so I can send back columns from the road.

We're going to shower in the train stations. It's a pretty good deal. For $4 they give you a sliver of soap, a towel and fifteen minutes of hot water. They use a timer. If you're still soapy when the bell goes off, you dig through your pants for another $4.

The showers are private and amazingly clean. Most U.S. airports have public showers. You can take one at Intercontinental in Houston.

Two years ago, Third Degree, Rusty and I did a more leisurely tour of Europe. We spent every other night on the train.

So I know I'm in for trouble. Third Degree and Rusty are jackhammer snorers, especially Third Degree.

One night on the last trip it got so bad that I left our first class compartment and escaped to a car packed with European college kids playing guitars, drinking beer and generally going nuts.

It was actually quieter in there. I found an empty seat and conked out.

I have to go now. I've got a train to catch.

Day One

OUTSIDE PARIS—In America, all we hear is bad news about Euro Disney. It's losing money. No one goes there. Wealthy oil sheiks from Saudi Arabia have to kick in millions to save Mickey Mouse's tail.

David Letterman calls it "Never-Never-Profit Land" and "Euro Disaster."

But here in France, twenty miles outside of Paris, Mickey, Donald and Snow White are putting on a brave face.

They're quick to admit that, sure, Euro Disney hasn't met financial expectations, but when Disney is involved, expectations run extremely high. Lost in all the bad news, the red ink and closed hotels is one simple fact: Euro Disney has become Europe's number one tourist attraction.

Strangely, attendance isn't the problem. Twenty-two million

customers have visited Euro Disney since it opened April 12, 1992. It's just that people aren't spending as much money as Disney expected once they're inside the park. They aren't buying mouse ears and duck hats and snow cones like they should.

That's because money is tight in Europe. And, as every parent who's ever been dragged through DisneyWorld knows, Minnie Mouse sweatshirts and Davy Crockett coonskin caps aren't cheap.

"Europe, all of Europe, has been going through hard financial times. We opened when Europe had nine consecutive semesters (quarters) of recession. It's affected all hotels and leisure companies," said Euro Disney spokeswoman Anne-Marie Carton.

Euro Disney is by no means giving up. Something plainly isn't working (net income at Walt Disney Co. was depressed last year by a $514.7 million charge associated with losses at Euro Disney), and they intend to fix it.

On Saturday, they changed the name of the place. No more Euro Disney. Now it's "Disneyland Paris."

"We find that people know more about Paris. The name has a magic touch that 'Euro Disney' doesn't have," Carton said.

Disneyland Paris is going to have a little more European style and flair. European chefs are being given a freer hand in the restaurants.

Euro Disney started as a carbon copy of an American Disney park, right down to street signs in English and rides based on American movies. Carton wouldn't say it was a mistake to jam American culture down French throats but, "We have to find things that are going to be loved by people here," she said.

Americans already may notice some differences. When I high-fived Goofy during the Main Street Parade, he gave me a big hearty "bon jour, h'yukh'yuk." Subtle stuff like that.

When I rode the mechanical bull, I swear the operator turned up the juice because I was an American. The French guy in front of me didn't fly nearly as far, and his backside probably doesn't hurt as much as mine does today.

The park wasn't as crowded as the Disneys in America. The Galleria shopping mall is busier—certainly with more young people. My wait to board the Indiana Jones Temple of Peril ride took only five minutes.

Donald Duck has a little larger role in Disneyland Paris than in America. "Northern Europeans prefer Donald Duck. Southern Europeans like Mickey Mouse the most. Overall, Mickey is still the favorite," Carton said.

Don't forget, Donald Duck cartoons were once banned in parts of Europe because Donald doesn't wear pants. A hat, sure. A sailor shirt, neatly pressed. Pants? None.

The Main Street Parade is called the Classic Parade. It marches four times a day: once in the morning, twice in the afternoon, once at night.

Disneyland Paris is hoping for a business jolt from "The Lion King" next month. That's when Disney's most popular movie of all time opens in Europe. There already is a Lion King float in the Classic Parade. Once the movie gets rolling, there will be Lion King everywhere.

In order to get visitors to spend more, Disneyland Paris has lowered prices on souvenirs and refreshments by thirty percent across the board. They're moving to inexpensive fast food joints instead of swanky French restaurants.

Admission is cheaper, too, although it's still quite expensive: $50 during summer, $45 in fall and spring and $35 in winter.

Disneyland Paris is open 365 days a year.

Disneyland in winter is something most Americans can't imagine. It's already chilly in Paris. By January, it will be bone-brittling, feet-freezing, below-zero cold.

Who's going to stand in line two hours for an 890-second, wind-whipping whirl in runny nose weather?

"Most of our attractions are covered. For the outdoor ones we have ways of keeping our guests entertained while they wait," Carton said.

To me, shivering may look like break dancing, but it's not entertainment.

"Plus in winter, the crowds are smaller so the waits are shorter," she said.

This month, Disneyland Paris is holding a Far West Festival, with appearances by "American country music stars," like Willie Nelson, Charlie McCoy, Billy Swan and Big Al Downing.

Big Al Who?

I'm no country music expert, but wasn't Al Downing the pitcher who served up Hank Aaron's 715th home run?

Disneyland Paris says give it time. Most theme parks take four or five years to show a profit. Remember, there's never been anything like Disneyland in Europe. It's all new to this continent.

"People may be reluctant to come at first, but when they leave, ninety-nine percent of them have smiles on their faces," Carton said. "We will have to wait until they tell other people about our product.

"We are always planning new things. We have just opened our 20,000 Leagues Under The Sea attraction. Last spring, we opened Storybook Land, which tells European fairy tales like Sleeping Beauty and The Little Mermaid in miniature.

"Next year, we will have a super Space Mountain, which will be bigger and hopefully better than the Space Mountains in your country."

Bigger and better?

"Well, we will benefit from the Space Mountain rides you have. We will have extra special effects."

Disneyland Paris is immaculate, just like DisneyWorld in Florida. It's just as much fun (more if you don't like crowds). The food is just as tasty.

The only trouble with Disneyland Paris is...it's in Paris.

Come January, where would you rather be: Frostbitten Paris or sunny, warm Florida? You'd have to be trés Goofy to pick Paris.

Day Two

AMSTERDAM—Only in Amsterdam can you live in the world's skinniest house, and it's probably the most normal place in the neighborhood.

"This is a rather unique street. There's a lot going on. I've gotten to where I don't think my house is so strange," said Teun Van Wely.

Van Wely's home stands four stories high and twenty feet deep.

But only seven feet wide. Barely.

Model Kate Moss would have to walk around sideways.

If Hakeem Olajuwon lay down on the floor to watch TV, he'd bang his head on the wall. Or stub his toe.

Actually, he could do both at the same time.

Van Wely's front lawn is a canal where a floating police station is anchored. "I don't like it, it ruins my view," Van Wely said.

One street over is Amsterdam's notorious Red Light District, where hundreds of half-dressed prostitutes sit behind glass doors like lamb chops on a supermarket meat counter.

Around the corner is the Billie Holiday bar, where patrons can drink the local beer, Amstel, or smoke backyard-grown marijuana or snack on "space cakes"—chocolate brownies laced with hashish.

Prostitution, marijuana and hashish are legal businesses in Amsterdam. There's even a museum devoted to marijuana.

That haze hanging over Amsterdam? It's not air pollution.

It's happy hour at the Billie Holiday Bar.

The menu carries a warning about space cakes. They take a couple of hours to kick in, so don't eat too many because you think nothing's happening. It will.

Farther down the street is the Museum of Torture, where tourists can touch a guillotine that once chopped off a man's head, or test drive an authentic rack used to tear a witch limb from limb.

The streets are crowded. It looks like a Grateful Dead concert just let out, and the Star Trek Convention is waiting to get in.

In the middle of all this craziness stands—just narrowly—Van Wely's skinniest house.

Not to be confused with the world's skinniest flower shop, which is down the corner.

Van Wely bought the house in 1989 for $190,000. The first thing he did was paint. The second was ask tour bus drivers to stop pointing it out as a landmark.

"I have had to disconnect the door buzzer because people always want to ask questions," Van Wely said.

Now he pleads with tourists to go bother the flower shop lady.

Van Wely's house, located at 26 Kloveniersburgwal St., was built in 1696. Why so skinny?

Back then, Kloveniersburgwal was the River Oaks Boulevard of Amsterdam. If you had money, that's where you lived.

The Trip Brothers had plenty of money. They controlled most of Europe's arms supply.

The Trip Brothers were slightly eccentric. (If you're rich, you're eccentric. If you're poor, you're just plain nuts.)

One day, a servant told the Trip Brothers, you know, I'd be happy to live in a house that's the size of your front door.

So the Trip Brothers chipped in and built him a house, you guessed it, the same size of their front door.

"It is a little strange living here," said Van Wely, who's also tall and thin. "It fits well for me because I am a writer and a thinker. You have to change the way you live. You have to give away many things before you can live here."

The first floor is his living room and kitchenette. The second floor is his bedroom. The third floor is another living room. The top floor is the guest bedroom.

All the rooms have hardwood floors, although wall-to-wall carpeting wouldn't cost much.

Decorating the world's skinniest house was a little tricky, Van Wely said. "You have to use light colors and beautiful things. You can't have clutter," he said.

He owns a television. Naturally, it isn't a wide-screen model.

"Of course I watch TV. I watch CNN from America," he laughed.

A corkscrew staircase takes Van Wely up and down. He's taken a tumble only twice.

"The worst problem I have is that the walls get wet in the winter and the front windows get icy," Van Wely said. That may be caused by the difference in the cold damp air outside and the warm dry air inside.

Or maybe it's because Van Wely's skinny house is scrunched between a liquor store and a Chinese travel agency.

A better bet is the funky smoke pouring out of the neighborhood bars.

Day Three

COPENHAGEN—When I was in the eighth grade, I think we took a field trip to the zoo. Or maybe the botanical gardens or planetarium. I can guarantee you we didn't take the school bus to watch hard-core pornographic films or hear a lecture about Marilyn Monroe's sex life.

I'm not sure Mom would have signed the parental release form.

Dad, on the other hand, not only would have signed, he would have volunteered to drive the school bus.

"We are much different in Copenhagen than in America. We are more than a little freer in our thinking about sex," said Ole Ege, curator of Europe's largest museum exclusively dedicated to pornography and eroticism. "We have schools take class trips from the eighth grade and older. I try to make this an educational experience for them. I get very positive cooperation from the Ministry of Education."

Ege, slim and goateed at fifty-two, proudly points to a two-page article in the Copenhagen newspaper headlined, "The Pioneer of Pornography."

"I do consider myself a pioneer because I am trying to keep the history of erotic material alive. Many young people think pornography was invented in Denmark in 1968. They do not understand the history of it," Ege said.

The Museum Erotica, located next door to Illums exclusive department store on the ritzy Kobmagergade shopping boulevard in Copenhagen, indeed shows extremely hard-core sex films.

It considers itself as important point of Copenhagen culture as the Danish Museum of Modern Art.

As does the Danish Visitors Board, which enthusiastically recommends Museum Erotica as a "don't miss" tourist attraction, right up there with the Little Mermaid.

While Ege and the Tourist Board are gung-ho about the Museum Erotica, the average shopper strolls by without giving a second look to photos of spectacularly endowed men and women in the ticket booth.

That's because sex is treated matter of factly in Denmark. In this case, it happens to be the facts of life.

In 1968, the publisher of Fanny Hill, a bawdy book first printed in 1749, was hauled into court on an obscenity charge. As a result, not only was Fanny Hill allowed back on the book shelves, the Danish Supreme Court struck down all laws restricting pornographic or obscene literature.

One year later, the Supreme Court was at it again, this time lifting restrictions against sexually explicit photos in magazines.

Denmark became the first country on Earth to officially legalize the erotic film, book and magazine industry. No longer was the X-rated world controlled by slimeballs and creeps. Now above-board business people, especially women who did most of the work, could make a buck with porno.

The only exception is child pornography. That's still a no-no, punishable by heavy fines and jail time.

Ege was so thrilled at "the liberation of 1968-69" that he took his lifetime collection of pornography and opened a museum. What he once hid under his bed has now made him a millionaire.

Gee, and my mother threw out all my baseball cards.

Today, more than 100,000 visitors a year pay $10 to gaze at ancient X-rated urns depicting sex among pharaohs as well as Madonna's latest shenanigans.

One crumbly Greek vase from 411 B.C. tells the story of a Spartan village where the women refused to make love with their husbands unless the men agreed to end a war.

Make love, not war. And you thought the hippies invented that?

Great moments in sex history are recreated by the same company that makes wax figures for Madame Tussaud's museums.

Ege has been a fan of sexually explicit material all his life. He started as a collector, moved into photography and eventually produced several pornographic films. Along the way he married and divorced three wives. The first wife left when Ege began his film career. The other two, well, it's a tough business to stay married in.

Despite his active social life, Ege managed to save enough money to open the Museum Erotica. He still plows profits into purchasing new films and nostalgia pieces.

His prized exhibit: A dress worn by Greta Garbo.

"I wanted to do this as a totally new concept. I don't consider this a dirty subject and I treat it with respect. I know of two other sex museums but they aren't very dignified, if you understand what I mean," Ege said. "Plus, they are much smaller than this."

Actually, the Museum Erotica is an elegant building, with four stories of polished wood floors and tasteful carpets. Ege pays $200,000 a year rent on the place. The museum has the look and feel of a distinguished art gallery, with gentle soft jazz playing in the background.

It's the subject matter—sex, sex and more sex—that would give his neighbors the willies in America.

Zoning or no zoning. Nobody wants to sell women's clothing next to a museum that has an entire room dedicated to the history of condoms.

Another room in the Museum Erotica traces the impact of venereal disease on world history. There's a pornographic puppet show. An exhibit of French postcards. There is a handwritten manuscript of a dirty limerick by the great Scottish poet Robert Burns.

Perhaps the most popular room lists, in excruciating detail, the sexual habits of show business celebrities, including Denmark's favorite children's storyteller, Hans Christian Andersen.

This room has whole walls for Charlie Chaplin and Marilyn Monroe.

Among the other celebrities Ege squeals on: James Dean, Joan Crawford, Duke Ellington, Clark Gable, W.C. Fields and even Adolf Hitler.

All of them have one thing in common.

No, not that.

They're all dead.

All the easier not to sue, my dear.

Day Four

BERLIN—The precious cost of freedom is getting cheaper by the day.

In fact, democracy in Berlin, once the most bitterly fought-over city in the world, has hit rock bottom.

Graffiti-covered chunks of the Berlin Wall aren't worth the concrete they're written on. Now pieces of the Great Divide are usually thrown in as freebies when you buy a "real" souvenir of Berlin.

Five years ago, when the Berlin Wall came crumbling down, the wide boulevards leading to the Brandenburg Gate were packed with wall chiselers and piece peddlers. They were getting twenty dollars for a sliver.

American department stores were importing whole slabs and selling pieces with "letters of authenticity."

Crowds in Germany, including tourists and journalists from the world over, were in a buying frenzy. I happened to be in Berlin that day and brought home a chunk the size of a football. My piece was from the East German side, pure white, with no spray paintings of "Rick was here, 1976!" or "Pink Floyd rules!"

I took my hunk of the Berlin Wall to a metalsmith who cut it into a hundred pieces which I dispersed around *The Houston Post* and a local radio station, KKBQ-FM (92.9), where I worked on the morning show.

Hundreds of vendors made a fortune that tumultuous week in November 1989.

Now, five years later, you'll see more action at a garage sale in Bellaire.

"It's like after a war. The west has squeezed us like a wet rag," said Gerd Glanze, one of the few Berlin Wall merchants still in business.

"I used to sell my pieces for $200. Today I am lucky to get three or four dollars. Only my special pieces are still valuable. I guarantee that my pieces of the wall are the real thing because I take pictures before I cut them."

For a couple of bucks extra, Glanze will throw in a photo of your piece of the wall before it was chopped away.

"When you buy from someone else, you can be getting anything. Who is to tell that he didn't chop it from the wall in front of his house?"

Glanze sells pieces from all three Berlin Walls: The small white one several meters inside East Berlin, plus both sides of the ten-foot high, thirty-mile-long stretch that became famous as the impenetrable separation between democracy and communism.

Glanze's souvenir stand is across the street from the old Reichstag, the Imperial Palace where Adolf Hitler governed the Third Reich.

In a few years, when the capital of Germany officially moves from Bonn to Berlin, the Reichstag will house the Bundestag, their version of our House of Representatives and Senate.

"When that happens, we will all be closed down. The business will be over," Glanze said.

Before the Wall came down, Glanze was an entertainer in East Berlin. Will he return to the stage?

"I do not know. This is something that God will have to decide," he said.

But for now, he's still hyping the historical impact of his wares.

"You see this spot you are standing on?" Glanze asked. "If you take two steps to me, you are now standing in Joseph Goebbels' office."

Glanze's most expensive pieces are from the area near Checkpoint Charlie, the crossing point where West Germans and tourists were permitted to enter East Germany for one-day visits.

If you buy enough from Glanze, he'll notarize your passport with the original rubber stamp from Checkpoint Charlie for free. If you just want the stamp, that'll be two dollars, please.

Down the street, you can get the same stamp for one dollar.

To show how things have changed, the Checkpoint Charlie building is abandoned.

The "You are entering the American sector sign" is still there for a photo opportunity. Next to it are Middle Eastern salesmen hawking lacquer boxes, Russian toys and out-of-date East German military hats.

You can get the whole commie uniform, jacket, pants, two shirts, belt and shoes for $50. Tailoring is not included.

A big seller is a toy model of the Trabant, the East German diesel guzzler that West Berliners blame for the cloud of air pollution that hovers over their city.

"We call it the East German Rolls-Royce," Glanze said.

By the way, the Brandenburg Gate was closed the day I visited Berlin.

Not because this week marks German Reunification Day. Or soon will be the fifth anniversary of the end of the Berlin Wall.

No. They were setting up seats for an Elton John concert.

Day Five

WARSAW—Our luck finally ran out in Poland.

Our ten cities in ten days tour was running like clockwork. Even the overnight train rides were a snap-once I learned to sleep through the roar of Reg "Third Degree" Burns' blanket-fluttering snoring.

But in Warsaw, our road trip hit a roadblock.

A very expensive stretch of misfortune.

Our original plan was to visit the world's largest flea market at Warsaw's soccer stadium and buy old U.S.S.R. army uniforms to goose-step around Houston for laughs.

The first thing we did, as we did in every country, was change fifty dollars into local currency to cover Egg McMuffin, Coke and pizza costs.

In France, fifty dollars got us about 490 francs. In Amsterdam, about seventy-five guilders. In Berlin, about seventy Deutschemarks.

But in Poland, I handed over fifty dollars and the guy behind the counter brought out a wheelbarrow of zlotys!

The exchange rate was 23,000-and-something zlotys for one U.S. dollar.

The weather was sunny. I had on new socks. I felt like a million zlotys!

Feeling like Thurston Howell III, I asked a tourist information director which way to the flea market. Take Number Two tram, she said.

We figured we'd pay for the ticket on the bus. After all, my wallet was bulging with zlotys. I had enough money to buy the darn bus. I single-handedly rocked the Polish stock market.

Not two minutes after boarding the broken-down bus, a security cop threw us off and demanded to see our tickets.

"We don't have any. We're going to pay the driver," we said in our best dumb tourist fake Polish accent.

"I must fine you. You must give me one million zlotys now," the cop said.

One million? That's pretty steep.

Luckily, I'm the kind of guy who carries at least a million zlotys. You know, walking-around money. I'm a spender. Those zlotys were burning a hole in my pocket.

I paid the million fine, called him every dirty name I hoped he didn't understand, and got back on the bus.

This time I bought a ticket—thirty zlotys round trip—in advance.

Five stops later, more dirty rotten luck. Somebody picked Rusty San Juan's pocket. He lost his wallet, $650 in U.S. money, credit cards, his Social Security card and his Continental frequent flyer I.D. card.

Since Poles make about $200 a month in wages, Rusty's pickpocket probably figured he deserves a vacation.

I said, "Rusty, look on the bright side. If the pickpocket flies Continental, you'll still get credit for his frequent flyer miles.

"Plus, you've had your pocket perfectly picked in Poland. That's not only a crime, it's a tongue-twister!"

Rusty laughed. Third Degree laughed. I laughed.

Then Rusty asked to borrow $150 and I stopped laughing.

Polish currency comes in denominations of 50, 100, 200, 500, 1,000, 2,000, 5,000, 10,000, 50,000, 100,000, 500,000, 1,000,000 and 2,000,000.

The 2,000,000-zloty bill may be the largest denomination single piece of currency in the world. Monopoly money doesn't go that high. Even my dentist doesn't carry that kind of cash.

Third Degree, who's an accountant, started calculating. A twenty-zloty bill measures about two by four inches and is worth approximately two-tenths of one U.S. penny.

For fifty dollars, you can get 25,000 of these bills.

I'm lousy at math, but I listen to Tom Tynan the Home Handyman on KTRH-AM (740). I think 25,000 bills are enough to wallpaper my bathroom. If that doesn't get me a photo spread in Houston Better Homes and Gardens, nothing will.

A tourist tip: Don't convert any more U.S. money to zlotys than you expect to spend in Poland. They won't change it back to U.S. dollars. And if you try to convert it to currency in the next country you visit, you'll get a bigger laugh from the cashier than Don Rickles ever got at Caesar's Palace.

We arrived at the world's largest flea market around ten a.m. I don't care how big a flea market you've ever been to. Compared to this, you were at a garage sale. The Warsaw flea market surrounds a 60,000-seat soccer stadium, fills the parking lot and covers all the steps.

Flea market baron Bogdan Tomaszewski opened the business in 1989, shortly after the U.S.S.R. fell apart. Gorby and Yeltsin had bigger problems than a Polish entrepreneur becoming a millionaire—that's a millionaire by American standards.

Each morning, rain, shine or snow, 365 days a year, Tomaszewski rents out 5,000 spaces. The charge for each space is forty-five dollars a month.

Third Degree is still busy figuring out how much it will cost to wallpaper my bathroom in zlotys, so you figure out how much money Tomaszewski is raking in.

"I do not ask them what they will sell here. I only ask them not to sell guns or narcotics," Tomaszewski said. "I have people who walk around and check for me to make sure nobody breaks the rules."

The Warsaw flea market has changed over the years. Back in 1989, most of the vendors were Russians selling cameras and binoculars to Polish customers.

Now seventy percent of the merchants are Polish selling goods to visiting Russians. Everything from caviar to mink coats to the anti-car-theft device, the Club.

They sell luggage, Spanish college sweatshirts, cellular phones, Hulk Hogan dolls, Russian passports, "Amerikanski" military uniforms, Gillette razors on the same table as Nazi war medals, portraits of Josef Stalin and jars of Paul Newman popcorn.

It costs sixty zlotys to use the restroom. Toilet paper is an additional fifty zlotys for four measly sheets of one-ply. Ain't capitalism grand?

Prices are dirt cheap. Thirty thousand customers jam the stadium during the off-season. The flea market opens at seven a.m., gets busy at eleven a.m. and closes by four p.m.

Billions and billions of zlotys change hands each day. If Bud Adams lived here, he'd want to build a domed flea market in downtown Warsaw.

I bought a German soccer shirt for $1.35 and a roasted chicken for $1.70.

"The Russians come here and buy 200 of my roast chickens and rush home and sell then for twice as much," the Chicken Lady said. "The Russians have lots of money, but they are poor because they have nothing to buy at home.

"In Poland now, we have things for them to buy. It's funny how things have changed."

Day Six

BUDAPEST—This city of centuries-old charm has inspiring church-
es, invigorating thermal baths, triumphant monuments to the over-
throw of communism and restaurants that make Hungarian goulash
like you will not believe.

But there was only one place on my must-see list in Budapest: 97
Andrassy Street.

The house where Zsa Zsa Gabor grew up.

Before I left for Europe, I called Zsa Zsa for the address. She did
better than that. She arranged for her cousin, Jozsef Gabor, to give me
a personalized tour of her childhood home.

"He will be happy to do it. He has the most gorgeous wife in the
world," Zsa Zsa said. Somehow, when Zsa Zsa said it, it made sense.

Zsa Zsa said she has vivid memories of the house even though
she lived there, as Betsy Parish says, "mumblesomething" years ago.

"I am an American now. I remember my home in Budapest was
very, very big. My father was a very wealthy man, a landowner, and
then he went into the jewelry business with my mother's family.

"The house was so big. The kitchen was bigger than my whole
house now in Bel-Air. To be honest, I didn't go in the kitchen much.
My mother didn't either. We had four workers who made our meals.
It was as big as a hotel kitchen.

"Look, darling, I don't go in my kitchen much now, so why
would I have done it then?"

Zsa Zsa shared "one big bedroom" with her older sister Magda
and younger sister Eva.

"I had a fantastic life growing up in that house. Like every little
girl, I had a secret hiding place. I used to hide under the piano with
my pet dog, a German shepherd named Lady. My father bought the
dog for me when I was six months old."

Zsa Zsa left home at fifteen when she married the Turkish

ambassador to Budapest. When she was seventeen, she came to America and three months later married hotel gazillionaire Conrad Hilton.

"But I still go back to Budapest every few years," Zsa Zsa said. "I will be there next month. If you can wait on your trip, I will show you the house myself."

Before I got her off the phone, I had to ask, "Exactly what does 'Zsa Zsa' mean?"

Zsa Zsa says her real name is Shari, "The same as Harry Belafonte's daughter," and Zsa Zsa is simply a cute name her mother made up.

Earlier, a member of the Hungarian Tourist Board said Zsa Zsa is the Hungarian equivalent of Susan.

Jozsef Gabor has a different story.

"Back when Zsa Zsa was a little baby, there was a famous actress in Hungary whose name was Zsa Zsa Fedak. One day, Zsa Zsa's mother was walking her in a baby carriage and they met this famous actress.

"The actress said what a beautiful baby Zsa Zsa was and she asked her mother, 'Why don't you call her Zsa Zsa like me?' Zsa Zsa's mother said yes and that's been her name ever since."

While Jozsef, who produces shows for Hungary's state-owned television system, was in a secret-telling mood, I asked, "How old is Zsa Zsa?"

"Ha! Now you are asking a family secret! I cannot tell you this. But I do know."

And what about the time she supposedly slapped the Beverly Hills cop in 1989? Do you think she did it?

"Oh, yes, I am sure. But if you or I hit a policeman, we just go to jail. When Zsa Zsa does it, it becomes a world scandal. That's the way she is. She is not an actress. She is a personality.

"Of course, later it became good publicity for her."

Despite Eva's success in the long-running situation comedy

Green Acres, Zsa Zsa remains the most popular Gabor sister in Budapest. For starters, Zsa Zsa won the Miss Hungary beauty pageant in 1936.

"We never received *Green Acres* here because America asked too much money for the show. We are more familiar with Zsa Zsa from her movies."

Like *Moulin Rouge* (1952), *The Girl In The Kremlin* (1957) and *Queen Of Outer Space* (1958). Of course, her autobiography, *My Story: How to Catch A Man, How To Keep A Man, How To Get Rid Of A Man*, also was published in Hungary.

"When the communists were here, the government renounced Zsa Zsa. They said she caused problems in the United States. She had too many husbands. She gave Hungary a bad name.

"But the people always loved Zsa Zsa. It was like everything else. The government said one thing and the people believed the other way. When she comes here and walks down the street, everybody looks at her. It is less with Eva. And with Magda, she is just rich and lives in Palm Springs," Jozsef said.

When Zsa Zsa comes to Budapest next month, she will stay with Jozsef, his "gorgeous wife" and their two children.

The family she'll recognize. The old neighborhood will look a lot different.

For example, the regal homes on Andrassy Street have been converted to foreign embassies. The Gabor house was one of the last to go.

It's a secret which country is moving in, but Zsa Zsa's old house is covered with scaffolding and filled with workers knocking down walls and uncrating office equipment.

The kitchen is gone (not that Zsa Zsa would notice). So is the bedroom she shared with her sisters.

Even her father's old jewelry store, the Diamond House, is closed.

"Things have changed here since the Russians left," Jozsef said.

"Land was cheap, even this big house where Zsa Zsa grew up. Today it is worth millions. So why not sell?

"I think Zsa Zsa will understand."

Day Seven

PRAGUE—Communism fell, officially, in Czechoslovakia on Nov. 17, 1989. The moment was celebrated in poignant historic ways. Free elections were scheduled. Young people looked for a better life than their parents. People were allowed to leave the country without waiting years for a visa.

Yes, there were big changes.

Most important, Grady Lloyd no longer had to wash his blue jeans in a bathtub.

Today, five years after the end of communism, Prague is a city on the move. Four hundred American corporations, including banks, restaurant chains, clothing stores and computer companies, conduct big business in the Czech capital.

The first American company to open in Prague, though, was a small coin-operated launderette called Laundry Kings, owned by a lovestruck Alabaman named Grady Lloyd.

"It was just timing. Grady was living in Prague at the time and he hated like hell to wash his jeans in the bathtub. He got here three days after the revolution," said David Orso, the current manager.

Grady Lloyd enjoyed life in Prague and wanted to stay. He had fallen in love with a Czech woman. The only thing that would make his world even more perfect would be fluff-dried blue jeans.

Does anything feel better than putting on jeans straight out of the dryer?

Laundry Kings was such a hit that Lloyd soon opened a second launderette. The coins started rolling in.

"Eastern Europeans have different laundry habits than people in

America," Orso said. "They have washing machines, but very few, if any, have a dryer in their apartment.

"So tourists needed a place like this. At the time, Prague was real popular with young Americans. The cheapest beer is here. Pilsener was invented in Prague, so you figure it out."

Prices are so good in Prague that McDonald's is one of the most expensive restaurants in town. Only tourists can afford to eat there.

"After Laundry Kings opened, Americans could just drop off their clothes and pick them up the next day. It was like anything else. We provided a service that nobody else was doing," Orso said.

Laundry Kings has twelve coin-operated machines. Or you can leave your clothes and have the staff do it.

Convenience costs. The washing machines are fifty cents, dryers are twenty cents for eight minutes. Shirts, on hangers, are fifty cents each.

Laundry Kings has a waiting room, a soda machine filled with American brands and a bulletin board pinned with notes from Americans looking for work, a baby sitter or a basketball game.

Growing ever more crowded with Americans (wearing clean clothes, thanks to Laundry Kings), Prague developed into THE city of Eastern Europe. The popular comparisons were, "It's Paris in the Twenties" and "Second chance city."

Sixty Minutes came and did a feature about YAPS—young Americans in Prague. That brought more YAPS, by the droves.

A rebellious English-language newspaper, *Prognosis*, began publishing a monthly edition in 1989.

"It was frustrating for tourists, especially the American community, to live in a city with no newspaper," senior editor Matt Welch said.

"Being young people, we didn't exactly craft a mission. We just wanted to publish a newspaper that we'd like reading."

Prognosis became a weekly newspaper in 1991.

"I admit that the name *Prognosis* is a pretty atrocious pun. In our defense, it was made up by five drunk people.

"We didn't want it to read like any other paper. *Prognosis* helped to make it sound new. Also, the pun indicated we were writing about the future of Prague."

Welch, sadly, thinks the future of Prague is past. He's planning to leave the paper in a few months and move to Macedonia, where the political climate is more "exciting." Plus, the "thrill" of starting a new newspaper is gone.

"After we started *Prognosis*, the business staff kind of revolted in 1991 and started a rival weekly newspaper called *The Prague Post*. I enjoyed the competition, especially because I think we do a better job."

Now a third English-language newspaper, this one a daily, is planning to hit the Prague streets next summer.

That will make three newspapers written by and for Americans in a former communist country where only 17,500 Americans live. And McDonald's is for rich people.

It's a wonder Paris survived the '20s.

Day Eight

MUNICH—First of all, Oktoberfest is held mostly in September for one single, easy-to-understand reason.

It's warmer in September.

And if you're going to drink yourself silly, eat too many greasy sausages, then jump on thrill rides painstakingly designed to make you puke, you might as well be comfortable.

That's pretty much Oktoberfest for you: The world's biggest beer blast.

How big? In just sixteen days, ending the first Sunday in October each year, Oktoberfest outdraws the Houston Astros, Oilers, Rockets, the Livestock Show and Rodeo and lawyers who've threatened to sue Wayne Dolcefino combined.

Oktoberfest started in 1810 to celebrate the wedding of Crown Prince Ludwig and Princess Therese von Sachsen-Hildburghaus.

They're still celebrating.

Oktoberfest is not a complicated festival. Each year, Munich's seven top breweries set up temporary beer halls a few blocks from the main train station. They throw up some portable rides, open a few games of chance (like knock down the metal milk cartons or burst the balloons) and grill a couple of bratwurst.

Then, oh, about 6.5 million visitors go berserk. It's the largest folk festival in the world. The Oktoberfest grounds are so crowded, you don't walk, you go with the flow. Fortunately, the flow eventually takes you to a bathroom.

Festival officials, all employees of the Munich Tourist Office, keep an amazing array of statistics regarding Oktoberfest.

For example, last year's 6.5 million visitors tapped 750,000 kegs of beer, ate 733,517 bratwursts and 224,547 pigs' knuckles. Eighty oxen gave their lives to Oktoberfest.

Overall, not counting locals, the festival attracted 5.9 million tourists to Munich.

Oktoberfest is held in the same place each year on a 100-acre site that goes unused the rest of the year. Everything is torn down.

Except those metal milk cartons. Nobody's ever been able to budge them.

The largest beer hall is the Hofbrauhaus, which seats more than 10,000 people. It's loud in there with live entertainment. You stand a mighty good chance of hearing an oom-pah band perform Rolling Stones songs.

You want to get tossed out? Try dancing on the tables. The waitresses will hustle you out physically and, trust me, they're more than up to the job. Hitler used to be a regular at the Hofbrauhaus.

Oktoberfest employs about 8,000 full-time workers and 4,000 temps.

Now for the important stuff: There are 678 *sitsplatze* (sit-down toilets) and more than 1,500 feet of standing-room-only urinals.

And still you have to wait to get in!

My favorite part of Oktoberfest is the amusement area. This is where the scariest, fastest, cookie-tossingest, loop-de-loop-de-est rides are found.

"All of the best rides are made in Europe and this is where they make their debut. People from festivals all over the world come to Oktoberfest to see what is the next big thing.

"They come from America and Russia and even India," said Max Zierer, who's traveled the world with his "Zipper" ride.

Get ready for "The Insider."

I'm still woozy. "The Insider" looks like a gigantic space spider who's just seen a can of Raid the size of the Empire State Building. It turns you upside down, inside out and around again. Two people fit in a car together. When the ride is over, you've switched sides. I've been on dates that didn't go this well.

It costs six Deutschemarks, about four dollars, to ride "The Insider." The Pepto-Bismol is extra.

"There are about four or five companies that make amusement rides in Germany," Zierer said. "Last year, the hot ride was the Olympic roller coaster, which turned you through five loops like the Olympic flag."

The year before was "The Topspin." In this business, you have to have something new every year. In three years, a ride is considered old already and nobody wants to ride it.

Zierer's expert advice when "The Insider" comes to America next year?

"Don't be foolish. The only bad experiences we have at Oktoberfest are young people, especially you Americans, who drink five or six beers and then go on the rides. Take it easy and you'll have no problem."

Day Nine

NICE—Are you like me? Do you fall asleep in cars and planes and buses?

And then you wake up with a brain-buster migraine from having your head rattle against the window for the past three hours?

That's how I feel this morning. Except we left Oktoberfest in Munich at seven p.m. and our train car looked like the drunk tank on Hill Street Blues. People were stumbling into us all night.

Plus, the ride to Nice took twelve hours. It was Animal House on wheels, dubbed in slurred German.

I am mentally, physically and cholesterolly exhausted from Oktoberfest. I never want to see another bratwurst as long as I live.

We've had a slight misdirection of destination for Day Nine. Originally we were going to spend the whole day in Monaco. But after poking our nose around Monaco and feeling out of place, we decided to go the extra twenty-five miles to Nice, the capital of the French Riviera.

That's because, after eight days of all-night train rides, we were in no shape, fashion-wise, for ritzy Monaco.

I was down to a pair of white pants (a no-no after Labor Day) and a Hawaiian shirt. Rusty looked like he just left Woodstock. Reg was wearing Bermuda shorts over sweat pants.

And I won't name names, but one of us isn't changing his socks as much as he should.

We were in no condition for Monaco.

And Monaco, where a typical citizen is a multimillionaire tennis pro who doesn't want to pay Swedish taxes, was not ready for us.

Last month, I asked the Monaco Tourist Bureau: "What's the weirdest tourist attraction you have?" I was looking for something unusual to write about, something other than the palace or the casino.

"As you know, we are a very small country. We are smaller than Central Park in New York City. But we have a car factory. That would be interesting," the spokesman said.

Sounds good to me.

Then he called back. The car factory closed down last year.

"I have another idea. We have no crime problem in Monaco, but we have a jail that is supposed to be very elegant. That might make an interesting story for you."

Hey, that sounds even better. Maybe I could spend a couple of hours in the Monaco jail and take a nap.

The police chief said nope. This isn't Mayberry and you aren't Otis. The Monaco jail is for crooks, not tourists.

I could have used the nap, too. Two nights ago, we gave up sleeping in couchettes on the train. Couchettes are bunk beds stacked three-high, six to a train car. Each bunk costs $24 a night extra.

So in Budapest we started sleeping, sitting up, in regular seats.

Here's a phrase you never hear at seven a.m. on a train: "I feel fresh as a daisy."

Nice is great. There's a bakery on Avenue Jean Medecin that makes the best almond croissants in the world. They bake pizza in wood-burning ovens on Rue Massena. They have a casino without a dress code on Promenade des Anglais.

If you have a satellite dish you can get CNN and American pro football.

For lunch, we hopped a fifteen-minute train to Cannes. I had a *pan bagnet* sandwich, invented in the French Riviera. It's tuna, lettuce, tomatoes and olives on a big crusty sourdough loaf. Rusty borrowed $5 (his wallet was lifted in Poland) and bought a *pan bagnet*, too. Reg went with a few almond croissants.

Back in Nice, Reg bought a copper bracelet guaranteed to ward off arthritis the rest of his life. As proof, the salesman showed a picture of Prince Rainier of Monaco wearing a similar copper bracelet. The salesman assured Reg that the prince does not have arthritis.

Reg wondered, "Did Princess Grace wear one of these, too?"

Tonight we hop a train for our last stop, Hamburg, Germany.

I'm supposed to meet the guy who runs the largest graveyard in the world. He should be loads of laughs.

Day Ten

HAMBURG—This is the perfect place to end our ten-cities-in-ten-days sprint across Europe.

Right after breakfast, we visited the world's largest cemetery. It's twice the size of Monaco and has 1.3 million souls resting in peace.

Ohlsdorf Cemetery also is Hamburg's Number One make-out spot for young lovers.

Then I got my Beatles fix by visiting the Kaiserkeller Club, the dumpy nightspot in Hamburg's Red Light District, where the early Beatles—John, Paul, George, Pete Best and Stuart Sutcliffe—played six hours a night, seven days a week, in 1960.

Our last stop was the ultimate weird museum: Abwasser und Sielmuseum, which houses an incredible collection of worthless junk plucked from Hamburg's sewer system.

Ohlsdorf Cemetery is patterned after an old English garden, with thousands and thousands of benches, trees and bushes. It's so large that two city buses have regular routes through the cemetery.

Even though the cemetery averages thirty funerals a day, Ohlsdorf is not a morbid place. Gravesites are hidden behind trees and bushes. If you didn't know it was a cemetery, you'd think it was a public park. Except you don't have to watch where you walk.

Dogs are not allowed.

Joggers and bicyclists cruise along paved paths. Young lovers come to Ohlsdorf to cuddle and kiss. It isn't as gruesome as it sounds.

"It is not unusual to have them sit on the bench and kiss. It is a tradition. Nobody cares. It is allowed," said Jens Bluemke, who works in the cemetery welcome center.

The cemetery is open from seven a.m. to ten p.m.

Ohlsdorf has 600 full-time employees, 200 summer workers and three hunters.

"Rabbits are a very big problem here. My father is one of the hunters we employ to get rid of them. He shot 2,300 rabbits last year," Bluemke said.

The million-plus souls in Ohlsdorf do not necessarily enjoy eternal rest. Families pay about $175 to rent burial space for twenty-five years. If the contract isn't renewed, the space can be re-rented to the next customer.

"The body is decomposed by this time and we are able to use the space and the box (coffin) again," Bluemke said.

Special sections of Ohlsdorf are maintained for soldiers killed during World War I and World War II.

"We have, of course, German soldiers and American soldiers. They are kept very far apart," Bluemke said.

The welcome center provides free maps, directions and guided tours. Surprisingly, for a cemetery with 1.3 million graves, Ohlsdorf has very few celebrity residents.

Probably the most famous remains are the father and sister of famous composer Johannes Brahms.

"This is a regular cemetery. You don't have to be famous or rich. It is very big, otherwise it is not special. Anybody can be buried here," Bluemke said.

◄►

Before the Beatles hit it big, they were a bar band playing crummy clubs in front of rowdy audiences in Hamburg. For fifty-eight nights in 1960, their home was the Kaiserkeller, at the end of Grosse Freiheit street in the St. Pauli district of Hamburg.

It's one of the wildest streets off the Reeperbahn, known immodestly as the "world's wickedest mile."

Grosse Freiheit means "great freedom" and they aren't kidding. One of the live sex theaters invites audience participation. Sure it's dangerous, but at least your relatives won't mind coming over to watch vacation slides.

If you saw *Backbeat*, the movie about the Beatles' days in Hamburg, most of the action took place at the Kaiserkeller. The theater has been renovated and renamed a few times. A plaque sign outside the ticket booth tells the Beatles' story.

Across the street is Gretl and Alfons' bar (bier shop). In 1960, weary, thirsty Beatles drank a lot of beer there, sometimes without paying.

In 1993, Paul McCartney's world tour played Hamburg and McCartney finally paid his beer tab.

The check is in the window, signed, "Paid in full, Paul McCartney."

The Abwasser und Sielmuseum, just a short walk from the Reeperbahn, is a monument to things accidentally flushed down the toilet or tossed into a sewer.

Most of this stuff deserved a watery grave.

The two-room museum is shaped like a real sewer and stands across the street from Hamburg's water purification plant.

"We send out the bad water and it comes back very clean...we hope," laughed sewer worker Udo Schroeder.

After signing the guest book, visitors gaze at displays of: lingerie, false teeth, someone named Richard John Walker's driver's license from England, an unsigned blood donor card, tires, soccer balls, wallets, one black shoe, umbrellas and credit cards.

Schroeder will give you a history lesson about Hamburg's sewers if you want it. I said no. You can also get a private tour of the stinky sewers. I didn't even bother saying no.

Two thousand visitors a year come to the Abwasser und Sielmuseum.

The best part of the museum? There's no entry fee.

A Visit to Vietnam

Twenty years ago this month, the last American fighting soldier, a sergeant from Oregon named Max Bielke, shipped out of Vietnam. Two years later, North Vietnamese tanks rolled into Saigon, the south surrendered, and the war was over.

Now the Socialist Republic of Vietnam is expecting, hoping for, even depending on, Americans to return. Only this time, leave your guns at home. Bring money.

While our government maintains an economic embargo of Vietnam, it is legal to visit the communist nation. So far, most American tourists have been either Vietnam War vets or business people preparing for the end of the embargo.

I recently spent eleven days in Vietnam. I didn't fight in the war. And I'm not going to open a hamburger joint in Hanoi.

I was just curious about what Vietnam looked like. The following will consist of impressions of Vietnam. Not the war, but the country that may become our next good friend in Southeast Asia.

◄ ►

There is a constant, frenzied traffic mess in downtown Hanoi. Except there are no cars. The traffic jam consists of thousands and thousands of bicycles, all heading for certain crackup at the corner of Hang Khai and Quang Trung.

But nobody crashes, even though they shut off the traffic signal years ago. With no cars, who needed a red light? People in Hanoi can't afford cars. They barely can afford twenty dollar two-wheelers made in Danang.

So everybody pedals in all kinds of weather. If it's raining, they ride with umbrellas. I asked a shopkeeper, "How do you keep the umbrella from blowing away or crumpling inside out? I've tried riding with an umbrella and I can't do it."

The woman said, "We ride very slowly. We are not so anxious to get where we're going."

Hanoi is a gloomy, surprisingly chilly, colorless city, where men wear Army-style caps and women wear straw cone hats. Both are available at souvenir shops for two dollars. Don't let them tell you they cost three.

Life happens on the street. Mothers wash their babies in the gutter. Old women boil noodles. Bike mechanics patch flats for twenty-five cents.

There is a dead end street where a dozen barbers—no waiting—cut hair for one dollar in the outdoors. I asked for a trim and practically got a crew cut. My barber didn't speak English, so I held my fingers an inch apart. He thought I meant cut it that short.

Fancy embroidered T-shirts with Ho Chi Minh's picture on the front and "Lift The Embargo" on the back cost three dollars in stores. They're only two dollars from the kid tapping on your bus window.

I asked one guide if Vietnam had a problem with AIDS.

"We have a saying: 'AIDS will kill you in ten years, but a jealous wife will kill you in ten minutes.'"

So Vietnamese men avoid AIDS by staying faithful to their wives?

"Of course not. We cheat on our wives. But we do it secretly."

◀▶

Vietnam is one of the world's poorest countries and Hanoi, its capital, is one of its poorest cities.

I met a teacher at the Government House restaurant. He has been teaching at the University of Hanoi for twenty-seven years. He has a master's degree. He makes fourteen dollars a month.

Outside, a guy is digging holes in the street for telephone poles. He makes thirty-five dollars a month.

The guy with the shovel is more important to Vietnam.

The professor shares a three-room house with his four children. The rent is one dollar a month. The electric bill is four dollars a month. It would be lower, but you know how kids are.

They keep leaving the two lights, two fans and one radio on when nobody's home.

◄►

It isn't easy for boy to meet girl when Dad doesn't own a car, there isn't a McDonald's in the whole country, you share a bedroom with both your grandparents, and the U.S. government won't let Bruce Springsteen perform at the Saigon Hard Rock Cafe.

But, somehow, boy still finds a way to meet girl in Vietnam.

They hold hands on China Beach, the old U.S. Army R&R resort. They drink Cokes at a sidewalk coffee shop. They go dancing at a downtown disco. They love movies, too, especially American movies.

I asked a government guide if *Good Morning Vietnam* was a hit in Vietnam.

"Yes, that movie was very popular here. Except we saw a much shorter version than you did," he said.

Vietnam is a very young country. More than half of its seventy-two million people are under age twenty. That means half the people weren't born yet when the last American fighting soldier left Vietnam.

Vietnamese teen-agers don't dwell on the war with America. "We learn about it in history class. That was so long ago," said Thuy, a seventeen-year-old student. Thuy just wishes America would open trade talks with Vietnam so Van Halen can come to Hanoi.

"That would be great," he said. "Van Halen is my favorite group.

We can see Vietnamese groups and some groups from France. But nothing would be as great as Van Halen."

On the tour bus, our guide says the most popular styles of music are classical, folk, Buddhist chants and theatrical. Privately he says, "That's tradition. Young people don't care about tradition. They like your rock'n'roll. If a young person goes to the opera he will be teased by his friends."

The guide remembers seeing "Negro bands from America" during the sixties in Saigon. "Maybe one day they will return," he said.

Vietnamese teens buy counterfeit rock 'n' roll tapes from Thailand. MTV, pirated from an Australian satellite, airs on the government TV station about one hour a month. No radio station plays rock 'n' roll.

I visited a teen night club, the Bach Dang, in Danang. The cover charge was 15,000 dong (about $1.50) and a frosty can of Truc Bach beer goes for thirty cents. The club was pitch black inside. A Vietnamese band, with a girl singer, performed "Diana" by Paul Anka as thick smoke covered the dance floor.

Lift the trade embargo!

By any standards, Saigon has an exciting night life. There are hundreds of discos and dark bars. Some of the more expensive discos, like the basement of the famed Floating Hotel, are off limits to locals, however.

For laughs, Vietnamese can visit the Apocalypse Now bar on Dong Du Street. That's a hangout for backpacking young Americans and strange people of unknown nationality. The walls are lined with posters for American anti-war movies. The juke box plays "Louie, Louie" every other song.

Teen-age prostitutes and drug dealers ply their trade on Dong Du Street.

In theory, Vietnam offers free education straight through college. You hear a lot of "in theory," about education, medicine, employment and food supply.

"The truth is, half of all teen-agers do not graduate from high school and most of them are unemployed," a government official said. "We have a problem with young people staying on the street doing nothing."

High schools are a good indicator of Vietnam's foreign policy. Ten years ago, students had to learn Russian as a foreign language. Now the mandatory foreign language is English.

◄►

The welcome mat is out for American tourists, but the door bell is broken and the front door sticks.

It's not easy getting into Vietnam and once you're there it's tough getting around.

Vietnam can't help part of the problem. During the Vietnam War, every bridge and major highway in the north was bombed. Now the sixty-one-mile trip from Haiphong Harbor to Hanoi takes four hours.

Highways are one-way streets. Since they share space with railroad tracks, when a train passes, highways become no-way.

A Yale University professor, who specializes in foreign policy, was surprised by how backward Vietnam is. "I expected the country to be where the United States was in the 1920s. But they're far worse off," he said. "I'd compare modern Vietnam to 1820s America. We saw workers cutting huge tree trunks with hand saws."

In 1988, our government said it was OK to travel to Vietnam. In 1991, U.S. travel agencies started arranging trips. An official trade embargo still is in effect, however. So, technically, you can go, but you can't spend more than $200. That includes everything: Meals, hotels, phone calls, souvenirs and anti-diarrhea medicine.

The limit is not as limiting as it sounds. Food is extremely cheap. Filet mignon dinner for two at a fancy restaurant costs $10. They have not heard about diet soda.

Hotel rooms are twenty to thirty dollars for two. The occasional rodent visitor does not count as an extra person.

Souvenirs are cheap. I bought a marble jewelry box, a couple of Viet Cong hats, a pair of fake Ray Ban sunglasses, some children's dolls and a pile of T-shirts for $40.

The United States does not have an embassy in Vietnam. So stay out of trouble.

Vietnamese cops will help you stay out of trouble. In Haiphong Harbor, American tourists cannot leave the fenced-in dock area after dark. In Danang, there is an eleven p.m. curfew. In Saigon, bed check is midnight.

Of course, you could extend curfew several hours by slipping the immigration officer a ten dollar bill.

Vietnam says the curfews are for our protection. They don't want wandering Americans to get lost or get mugged.

It also allows Vietnam to keep tabs on visitors. I met a young American who lives in Saigon and represents a South African travel company. "Vietnam loves to tell you how open the country is. But don't believe it. They watch you pretty close. They're watching us right now. It's no big deal. You get used to it," he said.

A separate entry card is required for each city you visit. When you arrive, you have forty-eight hours to register with local police. Some cities, Dalat for example, are closed to Americans. The usual excuse is "bad roads."

Most American visitors arrive prepaid with organized travel groups. It is possible for individuals to tour Vietnam but the red tape is mind boggling.

Americans are not allowed to rent cars. So you must hire a guide and a driver. The guide works for the government. The driver watches what the guide says.

Americans cannot use credit cards.

Public transportation is not the lap of luxury. The Hanoi-to-Saigon "Reunification Express" train takes fifty-eight hot, sweaty hours—unless it breaks down. It rarely doesn't break down.

People kill chickens and cook them in the aisles on the train. Bathrooms are so disgusting that passengers prefer using an open window.

Time Travel

HAVANA—Havana looks like it's stuck in the fifties. Rusted-out DeSotos with four different-sized tires bounce along pot-holed streets. If a family can afford a television, it's probably a black-and-white portable with tin foil hanging off the antenna.

Most of Cuba's time warp is unintentional, though. Only the Tropicana night club is supposed to look that way.

The notorious Tropicana is where Michael Corleone cut his Cuban deals in The Godfather II, where Carmen Miranda danced the cha-cha with fruit piled on her head, and where Ricky Ricardo worked before he split for America and fell in love with Lucy.

Where wealthy Americans came for Cuban rum and Cuban fun.

Since Fidel Castro took over, Cuba isn't what it used to be.

Except for the Tropicana. You'll swear you're back in the fifties. Before Castro. Before air conditioning came to the island.

These days, the nightclub is cleaned up and certainly toned down. No more live sex acts. No more prostitutes. No more weapons on the table.

But the girl dancers still shimmy in tiny bikinis with their tushies hanging out. They still wear outlandish hats shaped like massive chandeliers. Castro can tell the rest of Cuba to cut back on electricity, but at the Tropicana, the chandelier hats stay lit.

The rum still flows. The stage show is still slightly decadent, with 200 musicians, dancers and singers.

The Tropicana, which opened New Year's Eve 1939, is set in north Havana, beyond Diplomat Row on Fifth Avenue. It is an outdoor club, with enormous palm and moncillo trees to trap the stifling night air and stale cigarette smoke. Ventilation is poor on purpose. The whole idea is to make you sweat.

A night at the Tropicana isn't cheap. Tickets cost between $42 and $63, and that doesn't include food or drink. You can tip the waiter to get a closer seat. Rum cocktails are four dollars. A dish of ice cream is three dollars. A fish dinner is $15.

Here's where you'll find the only pay toilets in Cuba—fifty cents per visit.

The Tropicana holds 1,000 people. They stage two shows a night, six nights a week. The club makes a lot of money. But it doesn't go to the performers. The dancers make $200 a month. The stars get about $100 more.

I attended the early show on a Friday night. The opening act was a tribute to Nat King Cole, a popular headliner in the fifties.

A woman danced a tribute to Carmen Miranda, complete with melons and bananas on her head. It was the most fruit I saw in Cuba without a long line of people waiting to buy it.

The headline comic asked the crowd, "Do we have anybody from Argentina here tonight?" Fifty people shouted yes.

The comic asked, "And Canada?" A roar went up.

He skipped through most of Europe and Latin America. Each country brought an excited response.

Then he asked for the United States. Nothing.

And Cuba. Not a peep.

The Tropicana has an elaborate, crisscrossed stage with secret chutes and ladders for the dancers.

Neon lights introduce the acts. The performers make a dozen costume changes. The singers race through the audience. The orchestra seems to be playing in the trees.

The audience sits at narrow tables, like in Las Vegas, so you're jammed in with strangers. Between the heat and the crowd and too much rum, tempers are ready to burst.

At my table, a man asked another if he'd blow his cigarette smoke the other way.

The smoker said no, in fact, "I might have a cigar!"

Moments later, their wives had to pull them apart.

Both men were in their seventies.

◄ ►

You haven't lived until you've barreled ninety miles per hour down a pitch-black highway with a crazy Cuban taxi driver who's punching radio dials to find a song he likes. It would be a positive step for U.S.-Cuba relations if he'd at least glance at the road.

My hotel room that looked so ritzy in the "Come Visit Cuba" brochure doesn't have hot water. Twist the cold knob and you get salt water pumped directly from the Atlantic Ocean across the street.

"Salt water is no problem. Just keep your mouth shut in the shower," a hotel worker advised.

In Cuba, if you're an American, that's pretty smart advice outside the shower, too.

U.S. citizens can—and cannot—visit Cuba. They can because it's OK with Cuba. Just bring money. Travel agencies in Canada and Mexico will gladly sign you up for tours that include round-trip airfare from Toronto or Merida, transfers, hotel and two meals a day.

The thing to remember is, when you arrive at Jose Marti International Airport in Havana, ask the customs agent to please not stamp your passport.

That's because it's illegal for most U.S. citizens to visit Cuba. Only journalists, educators conducting research or people with relatives in Cuba may go with the State Department's blessing.

A travel embargo has been in effect since 1961, when America broke off diplomatic relations with Fidel Castro's island. Castro nationalized all in sight, kicked America out and we haven't returned.

Your visit could cost $250,000 in fines plus twelve years in prison. On the plus side, prison sentences usually include three meals a day.

Each year a few thousand Americans travel to Cuba, anyway. They go because they're curious. And there is little chance the State Department will prosecute innocent, although technically guilty, tourists.

To the State Department, Cuba is communism's last evil breath. It's a misguided country of consumer cutbacks, product shortages and profound poverty. My taxi ride was doubly scary, for example, because Cuba doesn't have enough oil to light its street lights.

But to travel agents north and south of us, Cuba is a "delightful cocktail of sun, rhythm and fun."

I like all three. So I went to Cuba the Canadian way, the long way.

I paid $280 for a ticket to Toronto, $75 for a layover hotel, $550 for the Cuba package, $140 extra for a single room, $90 tax, and $40 for something I still can't figure out.

We flew Cubana Airlines on a Russian airplane. Things are a little looser on Cubana Air. People passed around a bottle of Scotch. A woman was in the bathroom when we landed.

Havana looks like those yellow snapshots in your parents' photo album They still drive rattle-y DeSoto coupes whose odometers conked out a half-million miles ago. Cubans know how to keep a car running. Not quietly, but they go.

"We are very good mechanics," a Cuban tour guide laughed. He was being modest. Cuban mechanics are MacGyvers in overalls. They swap parts from rusted-out Volkswagens and broken-down Ladas, the affordable Russian hunk of junk.

One day it rained. I was so bored I walked into town and got a haircut. It cost fifty cents. I never left a nickel tip before.

Television has been cut back, too. Morning shows have been canceled because it costs money to light the studios and operate the cameras.

The two Cuban stations come on at noon, broadcast for two

hours, then disappear, with no warning, sometimes in the middle of a movie.

They return at seven p.m. You can watch a forgotten American movie with Spanish subtitles or a baseball game with players you never heard of. The picture is sort of fuzzy and the sound isn't very good.

It's very similar to watching cable television in America, except the picture doesn't go out when it rains.

◄ ►

My fifty-cent haircut in Havana wound up costing $20.50.

In clear English, I told the Cuban barber "just a trim." But he cut the top and sides too short, so I stopped him. I left Cuba looking like one of Cher's backup singers.

Back home, over the bathroom sink, I took some scissors and tried to even out the back. I cut too much.

Then I cut some more off the top. Then I evened out the back again.

Then I made an appointment with a Houston hair stylist. He gave me a haircut, plus a lecture about trusting foreign barbers who charge fifty cents.

Haircuts aren't the only bargains in Cuba. Cigarettes and rum are cheap, too. Especially to the thousands of Canadian tourists who populate the resort hotels.

In the hotel gift shop, cigarettes were $10 a carton. Rum was $6 for the good stuff.

In Canada, cigarettes are $55 a carton and the same bottle of rum costs $35.

"If I can just smoke and drink enough, this trip will pay for itself," said one bargain hunter from Toronto.

Canadians are big smokers. They lit up in the middle of dinner. They smoked during a volleyball game. They smoked in the swimming pool.

That's why you should eat dinner early in Cuba. By the time the Canadians reached dessert, the dining room looked like Oscar's poker party on *The Odd Couple*.

Tubby dogs and cats had free run of the hotel. No one chased them away. They begged for scraps in the restaurant. One puppy slept in my hotel room a couple of nights.

Cuba and the United States aren't talking, but you can mail postcards from there to here. Postcards are twenty-five cents, stamps a quarter. But if you're going to write funny stuff, mail them from the airport before you leave. Jokes about Castro won't leave the island.

Cuba tries to jam U.S. radio and television signals. But on a clear day, you can see *Geraldo*. I caught the episode where Geraldo discussed whether or not Elvis slept with his "mama."

If Cuba wants its people to dislike America, they shouldn't jam our TV, they should wire the country for cable.

Channel Two in Cuba is mostly news, baseball and speeches by Fidel Castro. Castro's speeches last four hours.

I had dinner with a European journalist assigned to Havana. His toughest job: Covering Fidel's speeches.

"He's boring. It's always the same old thing. Sometimes he waits three-and-a-half hours to get to drop a bombshell," the journalist said.

"Just when you think he's wrapping it up, he starts talking about something else and goes another half hour."

The sports anchor on Cuba's nightly news has a beard and a ponytail.

You can take pictures of anything except soldiers in uniforms, the airport and military installations.

It's not a good idea to take photos of Cubans waiting in line to buy food, though. They're embarrassed by the situation and will think you're making fun of them.

Radio stations do not play commercials. There is no advertising on billboards, either. A rare billboard by the beach will say, "The best suntan is achieved while exercising."

Resort hotels have hot and cold running salt water. Bring extra underwear. I washed my shorts in the sink and walked funny all day.

Weddings are free. Divorces cost $100.

4.

"Pick on Someone Your own Age!"

Good Night, Irene!

Tennis legend Bjorn Borg beat me something awful. I barely scored a point. Roy Emerson was drinking a beer, for gosh sakes, while he pummeled me. I never won a game off Evonne Goolagong. I have never beaten a famous tennis player.

Maybe I choke under pressure. Maybe I'm just star-struck. Whatever the reason, I lose quick, and I lose big.

But I was ready to stop my losing streak Monday when I played hard-hitting Irene Boylan of Dallas. She's in Houston to compete in a big-time United States Tennis Association tournament.

Despite Boylan's impressive career record, I felt confident I could beat her. I'm hitting the ball pretty well. I'm coming off a victory in the Fondren Tennis Club championship. I've been running to get in shape.

But mostly my confidence soared when a tournament official told me Boylan was eighty years old.

The match was set up for four p.m. at the Houston Racquet Club, where they're holding the USTA event, the National Senior Women's Clay Court Championships.

The weather was on my side. Monday was sunny, hot and sticky. Great! I'll run her into the ground. I'll hit short drop shots and then lob her. She'll poop out.

Come on, she's eighty years old. I was going to ask her, "Hey, Irene, got any cute great-granddaughters?"

So imagine my anger when I show up for the match and I find out Irene won't be eighty until July! She's only seventy-nine. That makes her a spring chicken in this tournament.

I plotted my whole game strategy for an octogenarian, not some kid in her seventies. My confidence went out the window.

Irene smelled fear in me. She had me rattled and she knew it. All her "Oh, Ken, I hate playing on a clay court," and "Ooh, you hit with topspin," was just a set up.

This was no seventy-nine-year-old granny baking cookies and worrying about Paul Berlin's future. No, this was a lean, mean, support-hose-wearing tennis machine. She was a shark.

Irene controlled the whole match. She ran me from side to side like a puppet. She hit drop shots. She had a slice backhand that bit into the clay court and skidded low. She made every point torture.

Irene was pretty amazing. Halfway through the match, my shirt was soaked with sweat, and she wasn't even breathing hard. At one point, she hit a cross-court winner and laughed at me. "Hey, pick on someone your own age," I yelled.

I didn't tank, though. I kicked my game into high gear, cheated only a little and eventually won. Good night, Irene!

As we shook hands over the net, Irene said. "Thanks for the workout. I didn't want to play too hard because I have my first-round match tomorrow."

Who's Matilda?

SYDNEY—Several years ago, when they ditched "God Save The Queen," and picked a new national anthem, Australians settled on "Advance Australia Fair.".

Well, actually a few no-fun types in the government did the picking "Advance Australia Fair" is a pompous melody with lots of brass instruments and hardly anybody knows all the words.

But, everybody knows the real national anthem of Australia is "Waltzing Matilda."

That's the song Australian soldiers marched to during World War II, Vietnam and the Gulf War. "Waltzing Matilda" is what they play at rugby and soccer games. And when Aussies get rip-roarin' drunk on Saturday night, you think they sing "Advance Australia Fair?" Heck, they can't sing it sober.

"Waltzing Matilda" is one of those songs that's in English, but it's hard to tell.

So I visited Professor G.A. Wilkes at the University of Sydney. He's taught Australian literature for forty years and wrote The Dictionary of Australian Colloquialisms.

"It's a very complicated song from around the turn of the century. A lot about 'Waltzing Matilda' is disputed. But I can tell you what I think," Wilkes said.

Once a jolly swagman camped by a billabong,
Under the shade of a coolabah tree.
And he sang as he watched and waited till his billy boiled,
"Who'll come a-waltzing Matilda with me?"

Wilkes said, "A swagman was like your hobo or bum. He carried a swag, which was all his possessions rolled up on the end of a stick. A billabong is a small ditch of water that's left after a river dries up. A coolabah is an ordinary gum tree. A billy was a tin can in which the swagmen would boil their tea.".

Waltzing Matilda, waltzing Matilda,
You'll come a-waltzing Matilda with me;
And he sang as he watched and waited till his billy boiled,
"Who'll come a-waltzing Matilda with me?"

After each verse, the chorus repeats the last two lines of the previous stanza.

"People have debated who Matilda is," Wilkes said. "In this case, Matilda is his swag. Waltzing is simply walking."

Down came a jumbuck to drink at that billabong,
Up jumped the swagman and grabbed him with glee.
And he sang as he stowed that jumbuck in his tucker bag,
"You'll come a-waltzing Matilda with me.".

"It gets easier to understand now," Wilkes said. "A jumbuck is a young sheep. A tucker bag is a sack where you keep food. The swagman is stealing the sheep. Waltzing Matilda means he plans to eat it later."

Up rode the squatter, mounted on his thoroughbred;.
Down came the troopers, one, two, three.
"What's that jolly jumbuck you've got in your tucker bag?
"You'll come a-waltzing Matilda with me."

"A squatter was a rich farmer. He's called the police who are about to arrest the swagman. Waltzing Matilda means they're hauling him off to jail," Wilkes said.

> *Up jumped the swagman and sprang into the billabong,*
> *"You'll never catch me alive," says he.*
> *His ghost can be heard as you pass by the billabong,*
> *"You'll come a-waltzing Matilda with me."*

"Our swagman chose to commit suicide rather than go to jail," Wilkes said. "This verse is sung softly and with sadness.
"Then you can resume drinking your beer."

Cut the Blistex

There is a distressing new trend in drive-through dining—combining fast-food restaurants, gas stations and twenty-four-hour convenience stores—and I want it stopped immediately.

I refuse to eat any cheeseburger that was prepared in the presence of *Gent* magazine.

The earliest versions of these all-in-one pit stops were built along major highways. The idea was to get long-haul drivers and family vacationers back on the road in pronto time. Fill up the gas tank, fill up the kids, hit the restroom and grab a box of Kleenex.

If you were really good, you never even turned off the motor.

But now I'm seeing these combo stores on normal street corners in Middle America. Hey, I still haven't recovered from Woolworth's going out of business. These fast-food-gas-convenience stores are going to do to Zeke and Ernie's fillin' station what the thirty-screen multiplex did to the downtown Bijou.

As Siskel and Ebert say, the balcony is closed. So's the rest of the theater.

Kids are going to miss Zeke and Ernie's, where they could fill their bicycle tires for free. Once the fillin' station shuts down, kids will have to pay twenty-five cents for air. I hate when they charge for air and water.

And what about the proprietors? I'm not worried about Ernie. He saved his money. But Zeke's another story. Let's face it, he's not exactly qualified for the executive retraining program at Boeing.

Repeat after me, Zeke: "You want fries with that?"

Too many things can go wrong with these fast-food petroleum

emporiums. Blistex should never be sold within fifty yards of "secret sauce." Ol' Zeke's eyesight isn't what it used to be.

I think fast-food restaurants should stand alone. I don't even like it when the Kentucky Fried Chicken store and Taco Bell touch in Terminal A at the airport.

When I'm on the road, I have no problem stopping at different places for my cheeseburgers and fuel. Chances are good you'll get gassed up at both places, anyway.

Are we really in that much of a hurry?

I don't need to throw a $10 bill in the slot and say: "I'm the red Geo Tracker at Pump 8. I'll have a Whopper, large fries, chocolate shake—and give me the change in unleaded."

I can think of only one advantage of combining fast-food restaurants and gas stations: the bathrooms. Fast-food places usually have clean bathrooms, and they don't make you lug a key chain the size of a tree trunk the way gas stations do. (And once you get in the gas-station bathroom, you wish the key hadn't worked.)

Gas stations are amazing. The office door is open, the cash register has the key lying right there, and nobody's looking. But the bathroom is locked tighter than Fort Knox.

He's OK, Who's OK?

We all have our quirks.

For example, my friend Reg "Third Degree" Burns eats his popcorn one piece at a time. He never shovels a handful in his mouth like everybody else in the theater.

"I think every kernel deserves to be chewed separately," Burns says.

Oprah Winfrey talked about quirks on her show recently. Oprah wanted to know when quirks stop being cute little aspects of someone's personality and turn into major problems.

Like the husband who insists that his dinner be served in alphabetical order, until one day his wife leaves him, between the asparagus and the broccoli.

Oprah had a psychiatrist who explained the difference between lovable kooks and unbearable pains in the butt.

I wrote down twenty of my quirks. Then I showed them to the famous psychiatrist, Dr. Stewart Fern of the Lee Mental Center in Fort Myers, Fla.

Up to now, I've considered myself one of the world's wonderfully normal people, the easiest person to get along with. One thing did surprise me. It took me only five minutes to think up twenty quirks.

Here they are:

1) I have never touched a cat. I'm not allergic to them. I just don't like them.

2) Even if I'm alone in my house, when I use the bathroom, I close the door and lock it.

3) I have never eaten Mexican food.

4) When I sleep, I like the ceiling fan and a portable fan blowing at hurricane force.

5) When I'm really bored, like during a speech, I'll write down every song on every Beatles album, in their correct order, just to see if I can still do it.

6) I waited in line for an hour so I'd be the first customer at the new Hooters.

7) I have never used a Port-o-Potty. I'd rather explode internally.

8) I have about fifty T-shirts, but I wear the same five or six over and over.

9) I have never called a radio talk show.

10) I have never watched *Star Trek*.

11) I have never gone to a health club. Never lifted a weight.

12) I eat dinner in order. Like at Thanksgiving, I'll eat all the peas, then all the mashed potatoes, then all the stuffing, then all the turkey.

13) I iron my jeans and T-shirts.

14) I have never had a beer. I have never been drunk.

15) I can't sleep in a quiet room. I have to have the radio on.

16) I have never seen one episode of *Star Trek* or any of the *Star Wars* movies.

17) I cook dinner for my dogs every night.

18) I have never heard a Garth Brooks record all the way through.

19) I have lost money betting against the Harlem Globetrotters.

20) Contrary to everybody else it seems, if I won the Texas Lottery, I'd quit my job immediately.

You know, I'm thinking I may be a lunatic. And that's without getting into my family stuff.

So what's the diagnosis, Dr. Fern?

"You may be the best adjusted person I've ever met," he said. "There's nothing frightening on your list. I have a ceiling fan and the air conditioner going full blast, too. And most important, nobody should ever use a Port-o-Potty if they can avoid it.

"You're fine, but that guy who eats popcorn one piece at a time? I think he needs therapy desperately."

A Day in the Life

Put it this way, the regular city bus tour of Liverpool takes forty-five minutes and leaves once a day.

The Beatles bus tour of Liverpool takes two hours, costs twice as much and departs twice a day.

They should put up a sign at City Hall: "For Beatles fans only."

The birthplace of the Beatles is a one-day trip from London. The train leaves Euston station at 10:20 a.m. and costs $50 round trip.

You arrive at Lime Street station at one p.m., plenty of time to run to Mathew Street and buy some authentic fake souvenirs from the basement Beatles Shop.

The cluttered store lies across the street from where the Cavern Club once stood. I bought a clock made from a "Hey Jude" forty-five and a key chain.

For bigger bucks, the Beatles Shop carries every song the group ever recorded, plus rare singles, photos and out-of-print albums. The bigger the fan you are, the broker you'll be when you leave.

After they tore down the Cavern Club, they built a shopping arcade That's where they have the "Four Lads Who Shook The World" statue. It takes a minute to see it.

The last "Magical History Bus Tour" rolls out from Merseyside Welcome Centre at 2:30 p.m. daily. Tickets are $7.50.

When the tour started in 1983, it ran once a week on Sunday morning. Five years ago I took the tour in a Volkswagen bus.

Now you ride comfortably in a double-decker bus with a guide, stereo sound system and air conditioning. The tour goes daily.

The bus takes you to landmarks like the registry office where John and Cynthia got married, past the restaurant where they celebrated (Brian Epstein paid), to the hospital where Julian was born.

You see the house where Paul learned to play piano, the school Ringo rarely attended and the street where John's mother was run over by a car.

You drive past Penny Lane, where the song comes to life. Here's the roundabout, the barber shop, the bank, the fire station and bus shelter. Everybody piles out of the bus to snap a picture by the street sign.

Something new is The Beatles Story museum at Albert Dock, Liverpool's answer to the San Antonio River Walk. (Except at Albert Dock, there's more Mexican restaurants.).

The Beatles Story is a loud, multimedia, walk-through labyrinth. The best room is a life-sized Cavern Club, redone to precise detail. You'll be surprised how small the stage was.

No surprise, the last stop is a souvenir store three times bigger than the Cavern Club. The souvenirs on Mathew Street are better and cheaper, however.

The Beatles Story is open every day of the year except Christmas. Admission is $7.50.

The last train back to London is at eight p.m. But you're far from done with the Beatles.

A play, *Glass Onion*, recently opened in Piccadilly Circus. It's a John Lennon look-alike performing Beatles songs. Don't bother.

Every Wednesday and Sunday, the Beatles Fan Club takes visitors on a walking tour of London.

The Wednesday tour meets at two p.m. at Tottenham Court Road Underground and visits the registry office where Paul and Linda were married and the court where John and Yoko were busted for drugs.

The Sunday tour leaves Baker Street Underground at eleven a.m. and passes Paul's business office, the Apple office and the famous rooftop where the Beatles played their last concert in public.

The tours are $6, a deal considering your guide just won the 1993 "Beatles Brain of Britain" contest.

The Heat is On

FINLAND—This morning, I spent fifteen minutes in a room hot enough to bake cinnamon rolls.

I took a Finnish sauna.

Don't ever confuse that rinky-dink sweatbox at your health club with an authentic Finnish sauna.

A Finnish sauna is serious heat, a Nolan Ryan fastball with high humidity. The Finns love their saunas. There are 1.5 million saunas in this Scandinavian country of only five million people.

You can't blame them for wanting to get warm. One-third of the country lies above the Arctic Circle. You hardly ever see the sun during winter's deep freeze.

Santa Claus lives here.

Nearly every home, apartment and hotel has a sauna. "Taking sauna" is a spiritual part of Finnish life. Families spend Christmas Eve together in the sauna. Businessmen hold meetings in a sauna. Parliament has a sauna in the basement. Before there were hospitals, mothers gave birth in a sauna. Men smoke meat in a sauna.

"Wait till you try it," said Marja S. Murray of the Finnish Tourist Board. "It is a wonderful, uniquely Finnish experience."

She explained that the word is pronounced "sow-na." The first syllable rhymes with "cow."

I explained that I happen to live in the world's biggest sauna— Houston. If I want to sweat like a pig in hot sticky air, I step outside.

My plane landed at Helsinki Airport at 8:30 a.m. By eleven, I was shvitzing in a hotel sauna.

Murray advised me to crank up the sauna all the way—to 100 degrees Centigrade—and give it about thirty minutes to get toasty.

Then I should take off all my clothes and prepare to relax like I've never relaxed before.

I'm no weatherman, but I know that 100 degrees Centigrade equals 212 degrees Fahrenheit. And 212 degrees equals the boiling point of water. I make macaroni and cheese in water that hot.

"Don't worry, you will love it," Murray teased. "It won't hurt you. Sauna is good for the circulation. It has many health benefits. To make it really hot, you bring in a bucket and throw ladles of water on the hot rocks."

I didn't wait for the sauna to hit boiling. I grabbed a local TV Guide to read and jumped in early.

A Finnish sauna will fool you, though. The thermometer said 40 Centigrade, about 100-and-something Fahrenheit, but it didn't feel hot.

Unimpressed, I went back to the TV Guide, which was giving me considerably more trouble than the sauna. The Finnish language is similar to Hungarian and nothing like Swedish or Norwegian, in which I might recognize a word or two.

Best I could make out, *Happy Days* is on at eight p.m., and it's the episode in which Fonzie moves in with the Cunninghams.

At 115 Fahrenheit, it was getting warm, but a dry heat, nothing I couldn't handle. Not to brag, but my first summer in Houston, I drove a car without air conditioning. I'm tough.

At 140 degrees, I'm not so tough. Sweat was pouring down my face, my back, legs, even my feet.

That's when I threw a ladle of water on the red-hot coals.

Whoosh! The sauna filled with burning steam like Old Faithful just blew.

It's true what they say. It is the humidity, not the heat.

The thermometer hit 160, 180, 200, boiling!

I leaped out of the sauna like a rodeo bull out of chute No. 2. Unlike the Finns, I didn't race down to a chilly lake for a Nestea plunge.

Instead, I collapsed in a chair, tried to catch my breath, and deep down I knew a mistake had been made.

Fonzie never should have moved in with the Cunninghams. 🌱

Hulk Hoffman

My debut as a professional wrestler did not go as planned Saturday night at the Humble Bingo Hall.

Long story short, I was carried out of the ring on a stretcher. (By the way, the Bingo Hall needs to replace some light bulbs in the ceiling.)

I picked a wild night. It was the biggest wrestling show in Humble history. The Bingo Hall was rocking. Every ticket was sold, plus standing room only. Fans were scrambling for seats.

I arrived at the arena with my entourage at six p.m. I would have been there at five, like I was supposed to, but my trainer, Reg (Drew Bundini) Burns made me pull into Brown Sugar's Barbecue on I-45 so he could have a double chicken-fried steak with extra cream gravy.

My personal valet, the fantastic Alisa Wong (Miss Hooters, Kirby location) got there at seven p.m. She wore spiked heels and a slinky cocktail dress with sequins.

Uh-oh, big problem. I was wearing a sequined wrestling robe.

I never had to worry about my wardrobe clashing with a Hooters Girl before.

My opponent was the Jester, some clown from England with a snooty attitude. The guest referee was Top Gun Jag, who promised to call the match on the "up 'n up."

I should have known something was "up" when I saw Jag high-fivin' the Jester in the parking lot.

The Jester entered the ring first. He grabbed the microphone and did his usual shtick of mocking the local "Hill Williams." He said that Houstonians "go to their family reunions to meet chicks," and that Houstonians refer to the second grade as "my senior year."

You might be English if . . . you rip off Jeff Foxworthy jokes.

Then my entrance music blared. I picked "Help!" by the Beatles. It's got a good beat. And I'm about to get a good beating.

I wore something old (an Astros T-shirt), something new (elbow pads) something borrowed (the Terminator's patent leather boots) and something black and blue (my body).

I wore three pairs of underpants for extra padding.

The Jester taunted me in the ring. He said he's read my columns and my trivia questions have been too easy lately. He told Alisa to dump me and find out "what a real man is like."

Some real man, the Jester. He's wearing a hat with bells.

The Jester didn't wait for the match to start. He attacked me as I was kneeling in my corner, softly praying. He planted a size fifteen boot in my back. My head smacked into the turnbuckle.

Memo to the Humble Bingo Hall: more padding for the turnbuckle.

The Jester choked me, kicked me, punched me. The referee did nothing to stop him. You know, something really needs to be done about the quality of officiating in professional wrestling.

The Jester hoisted me into air and body-slammed me. While I was upside down, I noticed Channel 2 general manager Steve ("Let me hear from you") Wasserman in the crowd. I was going to wave hello to him, but I was too busy shrieking for dear life.

My friend Mike Davis, who works for a hotel, sprang onto the ring apron to protest. The referee cold-cocked him.

My neighbor James Rivera, a computer geek, flew into the ring and got in the ref's face.

Rivera woke up with a limp on Sunday.

I was hoping that Steve Wasserman didn't get any brave ideas.

The Jester hit me with a frog splash off the top rope, an elbow smash, a leg drop, an eye rake and several illegal chokes.

The Jester tossed a metal chair into the ring, and it was time for the coup de grace, the dreaded DDT.

Nobody gets up from a DDT.

The Jester kicked me in the groinal area and crashed me headfirst into the chair. That was the last thing I remember.

I'm told that several wrestlers, including former cruiserweight champion Wichita Willie, the Terminator (he probably just wanted his boots back), Sid Sexy and Johnny Blade rushed to the ring with a stretcher. They spent fifteen minutes securing me to the stretcher, making sure my spine and neck were immobilized.

Even though I was semi-conscious, I'll never forget the inspiring words of an innocent little boy, he couldn't have been older than ten, as I was carried to the dressing room:

"Hey, I came here to watch wrestling, not *E.R.*!"

The Perfect Gift

You can eat off my kitchen floor. Go ahead, invite some friends, too. There's enough food down there.

I've got pizza crust crumbs, spaghetti sauce splotches, Pepsi puddles, toast scrapings, a French fry or two, dog biscuit crunchies and chocolate dust bunnies.

I'm listed in the Zagat Guide for Roaches. I've got bugs with bulimia. When I turn on the kitchen light at midnight, my bugs don't run for the hills, they look at me and burp.

That's why I had to get the PVA 10X Mop. As Seen On TV.

The PVA 10X Mop is the latest, greatest breakthrough in kitchen mop technology. PVA stands for "powerful vacuum action." 10X mean it cleans your floor 10 times faster than ordinary sponge mops.

The PVA 10X uses super-absorbent, space-age material to suck up messes in a blink of an eye. Ridges in the mop collect dry particles like a magnet, so you're really sweeping and mopping in one swift, easy motion.

The patented "One Finger Ringer" forces every speck of dirt, grime and bacteria out of the mop and into the bucket where it belongs.

Personally I never use a bucket. I squeegee it right into the sink.

The PVA 10X Mop infomercial is dazzling, one of my favorites of all time. The host, a snooty British dandy, throws everything on the kitchen floor but the kitchen sink. Then he makes one pass with the PVA 10X and the floor is sparkling clean.

By the way, I have noticed an alarming trend toward sleazy British hosts on infomercials. Why can't they hire sleazy Americans?

The PVA 10X swoops up dust, stray buttons, ketchup and soda.

Shoes are not safe. The audience sits stunned, mouths agape, which makes it easier for them to swallow the host's spiel.

When audience members were told they could buy this high-tech gizmo mop for only $39.90 (plus $9.95 shipping and handling), well, their chins hit the floor. Luckily, the floor was immaculate.

On the surface, any surface really, the PVA 10X is a nifty good deal. It comes with a lifetime guarantee. If it ever cracks or breaks, send it back. If it molds or mildews, send it back.

It's even guaranteed never to smell funky. I wish my baby had that kind of guarantee.

Now I'm a tough one to please when it comes to mops. I was one of the first to buy the Miracle Mop, also As Seen On TV.

The Miracle Mop was packed with flaws. It would get all twisty and impossible to untangle. It was tough to wring out. Eventually it reeked something awful. I had to keep it outside in the back yard, next to my broken wheelbarrow and rusted barbecue grill. I convinced my neighbors that this junk was modern lawn art, my statement about declining suburbia.

I'm happy to report that the PVA 10X Mop is an effective floor cleaner. You can wring it bone dry with one finger. It's not so good at sweeping and mopping at the same time, though. You'll get streaks of wet, sticky dust. Yuck.

I've always found it best to vacuum the kitchen floor before mopping. That way, when your dog runs through the house with muddy feet, his paw prints show up really well.

If you order right away (in infomercial lingo that means any time before the Earth spins off its axis and hurtles into the sun), they'll throw in an extra mop for free.

My recommendation: The PVA 10X Mop lives up to most of its claims. If you need a new mop, I say get it. And give the bonus mop to a messy friend or loved one.

Mops always make great gifts. Especially on wedding anniversaries. Mops show you care.

Looking Up
Down Under

THE OUTBACK—Australia's most breathtaking tourist attraction is free, and the directions are so simple, even "bloody Yanks" who drive on the wrong side can find it.

Just look up.

The pitch-black sky in the Southern Hemisphere is more than a starry, starry night. It's planets, satellites, shooting stars, the real-life zodiac and a moon you can read by.

This is the place to go stargazing. If you crisscrossed the Australian continent, you'd hit Ayers Rock in the center. It's a tiny village next to a national park surrounded by Aboriginal holy land, deep, deep into the outback.

In other words, there ain't a lot of people here.

You can go on a star voyage with a National Park ranger or take a guided tour with a professional astronomer.

Shortly before sundown, we drove seven miles into the "bush," the geographic middle of nowhere. In every direction there was only undisturbed horizon.

As night fell, the only sounds were our kerosene lanterns, slimy desert bugs, lizards and other disgusting creatures. "I want you to close your eyes. I'm going to turn off the lamps. You should concentrate on the sounds," said astronomer Michael Lane. "It will be the first time you've heard what nature sounds like without cars honking and TV sets in the background. Then open your eyes and look to the sky."

It was the most incredible thing I ever saw without Steven Spielberg being involved.

The sky was darker than I had ever seen. More twinkling stars than I had ever seen.

Lane explained the difference between Australia's spangled sky and what happens when you look up in Houston. "The best place to look at stars is the Southern hemisphere. This is not me being arrogant as an astronomer. This is a fact," he said.

"Because of the way the Earth is tilted, the Southern Hemisphere looks back into the middle of the Milky Way, our galaxy. The Northern Hemisphere looks over the edge of the Milky Way."

So stars burn more brilliantly below the equator. But there's much more.

"I am guessing that Houston has air pollution and humidity. That cuts down on visibility. And does Houston have many lights, like neon advertising? That would make it harder, too," Lane said.

Does Houston have neon signs? Until I met Lane, I thought the golden arches at McDonald's were a constellation.

"Central Australia doesn't have pollution and the atmosphere is thinner. I personally think this place, and the highlands of South America, are the best places in the world to look at stars," Lane said.

How many stars can you see?

"If you tried to count them, you will forget what number you're on before you finish. Even without a telescope, you can see thousands," Lane said.

It really gets interesting with a telescope, though. We saw Saturn and its rings, clear as a bell. "The image is so good that people always accuse me of having a photo slide in the telescope," Lane said. "But that's the real thing."

Except Saturn's rings ran top to bottom instead of around the middle.

"You're used to seeing pictures of Saturn taken in North America," Lane said.

The moon looked like a golf ball that's been whacked too many times, all pitted out and dented. We saw spy satellites and assorted "space junk" streaking across the sky.

With a telescope in Australia, you can practically read the Space Shuttle's license plate.

One time in Houston, I thought I saw Saturn's rings, but it was only Wayne Dolcefino eating doughnuts aboard the Channel 13 helicopter.

Using a pocket searchlight, Lane showed us Pisces, Aquarius, Capricorn and more horoscope signs. You can see only six zodiac formations at one time. The other six are in the northern sky.

The Southern Cross was up there.

Lane conducts stargazing tours six nights a week, yet he seemed as excited as the tourists. "I'm always finding new things up there. I have the same reaction as you did tonight—awe. It's supposed to make you feel small. It should make people realize how small and fragile we are."

The Tea is Free

BANGKOK—Last week, I tagged along with a tour group in Bangkok, Thailand. I'm no fan of tour groups. You wind up seeing things you don't want to see and visiting places you don't want to visit.

With people you don't want to be with.

So one day, while the group went to an art museum or something equally boring, another malcontent and I sneaked away, hopped in a taxi and had lunch at "The World's Biggest Restaurant."

The world's biggest anything—that's my idea of a tourist attraction.

The Royal Dragon restaurant is about ten miles from downtown Bangkok, which takes more than an hour in the city's wretched, gridlock traffic. But cabs are cheap. The ride each way costs $10. For another $10, the driver will wait in the parking lot while you eat.

The Royal Dragon, which made the *Guinness Book of World Records* in 1992, is a Chinese restaurant owned by twelve Thais. The food is good. The statistics are mind-boggling.

The restaurant consists of eighty-four separate dining rooms, spread over twenty-two acres. The bad news is that forty of the rooms feature karaoke machines. There is a distinct possibility you'll be treated to Fred Tourist from Minneapolis singing "My Way."

The Royal Dragon can handle 5,000 guests at one seating and usually serves 10,000 meals a day. There's no such thing as a power table. Well, there may be one where you can't hear Fred croaking "My Way."

Other music rooms feature live concerts by famous Thai singers such as Ruangthuoung Thonglanthom and Tharthip Srisawat. They may be hard to pronounce, but they do take requests.

One room is shaped like a fishing boat. It's moored in an enormous swimming pool stocked with live fish. You can dine inside, outside or on the roof.

The parking lot holds about 1,000 cars and buses. Uniformed traffic cops keep things moving.

There are four far-flung kitchens. On a busy Saturday night, the full staff of 322 cooks is on duty, whomping up Chinese, seafood, Thai and European meals.

I started with a bowl of corn soup, Chinese-style, for $2, passing on the Tum Yum fried pig knuckle with chili, lime and condiment soup.

The Royal Dragon menu is a colorful, photo-packed encyclopedia of food, ranging from the simple (fried rice) to yucky (Chinese pickle and pork tripe consommé). If it walks or crawls, or if you can bread it and fry it, it's most likely on the menu.

The menu has several pages of advertising. A pack of Thai cigarettes goes for $1.15. Matches cost extra. Toothpicks are free, and it's not poor manners to use them right at the table.

Soup is prepared in the outer-limits kitchen, more than nine football fields from the main dining room. Still it arrived steaming hot, not a drop spilled, thanks to my speed-demon waiter on roller skates.

All the waiters wear Chinese silk pajamas and revved-up skates. The restaurant guarantees that your food will travel from kitchen to table in less than two minutes. The waiters move faster than Tennessee Oilers receivers, and they don't fumble.

During lunch and dinner, the restaurant looks like a roller derby match with no referee. Miraculously, nobody crashes.

In the middle of the complex stands the seven-story Muen Pee Tower. If you're sitting at a lucky table, your waiter will climb to the top, hook himself to a trapeze and deliver your food like the Flying Santoni Brothers. The flying waiters dress like Batman.

Other waiters don floating shoes and walk across the swimming pool to deliver your food.

The total kitchen and wait staff tops 1,000 people, all of whom are provided free on-site housing. It's not lavish, but they get to work on time. Even the manager lives out back.

The Royal Dragon uses 46,000 plates and dishes a day, plus 34,564 forks and spoons.

This may be a Chinese restaurant, but as in a Thai restaurant, knives are not used.

Every night at 7:30 and 10:30, there's a traditional Thai dancing program. The Royal Dragon is loud, raucous and noisy. It's not recommended for first dates.

Last dates, maybe.

My main course was fried rice with egg for twenty cents. My buddy had steamed grouper (head on) for $3. Tea was free. My diet Coke was fifty cents with free refills. You gotta like these prices.

On the negative side, the restrooms are so far away, you feel like packing a lunch. But as in a classy restaurant, there is no advertising by limousine companies over the urinals.

At any one time, the restaurant is serving twelve tour buses of German tourists, a high school reunion, three weddings, a couple thousand stragglers and hundreds of karaoke crooners. The restaurant serves dinner up to eleven p.m., and the karaoke rooms stay open until two a.m.

If you can't finish dinner—and the portions are gargantuan—your waiter will pack up the leftovers in familiar white cartons. If you happen to live in the neighborhood, sorry, the Royal Dragon doesn't deliver.

Boy-o-Boy-ar-dee!

OVER THE weekend, while bicycling to get bagels, a group of us played a game called "Dead Or Alive."

That's where somebody says the name of a celebrity who's sort of forgotten, and you have to guess whether he's dead or still alive.

For example: Fats Domino (alive), Ray Walston (alive), Spiro Agnew (dead), Roger Maris (dead), Mickey Rooney (alive) and Mr. Ed (dead).

Then someone said, "Chef Boy-ar-dee."

I guessed alive.

Nope, dead.

I was crushed. I loved Chef Boy-ar-dee, especially his ravioli. I must have eaten a ton of Chef Boy-ar-dee when I was growing up. If Mom called and said she was working late, no problem, I just opened a can of ravioli for supper.

I knew Chef Boy-ar-dee was a real person because I saw him interviewed on television once. I even knew his first name: Hector.

I had to find out if Chef Boy-ar-dee was really dead.

I tracked down the company that makes Chef Boy-ar-dee ravioli and talked to the president.

"I hate to break the news to you, but I'm afraid the Chef is no longer with us," said Charles LaRosa of American Home Food Products in Madison, N.J.

Chef Boy-ar-dee died in 1985. He was eighty-seven.

He was a pretty remarkable man in more ways than ravioli.

Hector Boiardi grew up in the northern Italian town of Piacenza. He went to work in restaurants and hotels at age eleven.

His older brother Paul urged Hector to come to America in 1915.

Hector's skill with a skillet gained a fast reputation and he was hired by New York's swankiest restaurants. He catered President Woodrow Wilson's wedding at the Greenbriar Hotel in West Virginia.

"Right after that, Hector moved to Cleveland and opened his own restaurant, Il Giardino d'Italia. It was an immediate hit," LaRosa said.

That's putting it mildly.

Not only was the joint packed nightly, the kitchen worked overtime preparing takeout "spaghetti dinner kits."

Boiardi asked the customers how many people would be eating, then he poured the precise amount of sauce into old milk bottles. He tucked in a pack of cheese and a handful of uncooked spaghetti.

His famous Italian Spaghetti Dinner, exactly as it's sold today, was born. The takeout business expanded and boomed. At the height of the Great Depression, Boiardi had three food plants working around the clock.

He decided to name his product line Chef Boy-ar-dee Quality Foods because customers had a tough time spelling Boiardi.

In 1938, Boiardi shut down the Cleveland operation and moved to Milton, Pa. He built a huge factory and bought enough land to grow his own tomatoes.

When World War II started, Boiardi stopped selling to stores and sent all his food to U.S. troops fighting overseas.

"American Home Foods made the Chef a wonderful offer in 1948 and we bought the company," LaRosa said. "Of course, we wouldn't have bought it unless he agreed to stay with us as a lifelong adviser."

Today, Chef Boy-ar-dee is a $700 million-a-year global enterprise. Every label still bears his friendly crinkly face and trusty chef's hat.

"One of the unique things about Chef Boy-ar-dee is that his picture on the label aged with him," LaRosa said.

"If you were a kid in the '50s, you probably remember him with black hair and a nice dark mustache. Children from the '60s know him a little older. Today's kids see him with white hair. The last picture, the one we use now, was taken when he was about seventy-five."

Sweet Defeat

If anybody's counting, the Washington Generals' losing streak is now at 14,204.

The Harlem Globetrotters beat the Generals 82-67 Saturday in front of 11,034 fans at The Summit.

I didn't single-handedly lose the game for the Generals. But my oh-for-three shooting and lazy defense didn't help. On the plus side, nobody on the Globetrotters pulled down my pants.

This was my third year as guest General in Houston. I'm 0-3. But I'm way ahead of Coach John Farrero. He's oh-for-fourteen years.

"Who's counting? We play 200 games a year and I've never won one. I hope the team owner doesn't fire me," he laughed.

Farrero is safe. The team owner is his father-in-law, Red Klotz, whose record as coach is only a little better. Klotz has three wins.

Klotz also has forty-one years worth of losses.

The Generals, as bad as they are, need two coaches because there usually are two groups of Globetrotters on the road. The Generals aren't millionaire first-round draft choices. No, they come from schools like Alfred University and Bloomberg College. They're too short and too slow.

One time in Houston, the Generals center didn't play because he ate fifteen pieces of fried chicken on the team bus and got sick.

Farrero remembered me from last year. "You know the routines, right? We'll do the same plays."

I started the second quarter. The Generals already were down by thirteen points. On our first possession, I set up near the three-point line. I dribbled once and shot. Air ball.

On our second possession, I got the ball in the same spot. But this time, Globetrotter Sweet Lou Dunbar fouled me.

I wanted to shoot the foul shots fast, before Dunbar could ask me embarrassing questions.

No luck. The ref, who was totally partial to the Trotters, held the ball until Dunbar could size me up. He mentioned something about leaping ability.

My first shot rattled off the rim.

"Try a little closer," Dunbar said. He lifted me up and plopped me two feet from the hoop.

I missed again.

It's not easy playing in front of a big crowd at The Summit. Just ask the Houston Rockets. Ask Michael Jackson next time he comes to Houston.

And it's not easy to shoot a basketball that's coated with sticky goo. It's so the Globetrotters can work their sleight of hand. Another secret. Of course, the Generals must steer clear when the Trotters go into a famous bit, like when Dunbar rummages through a fan's purse.

But if the Trotters mess up a routine, even for a second, the Generals can play honest-to-goodness defense. The Generals love it when the Trotters goof.

"Just once, I want to get the Globetrotters in a real game. We could play in a gym at midnight, with real refs, in front of no fans," Farrero said. "I really think we'd beat them."

Truth is, a decent high school team could beat the Globetrotters. Five guys from the schoolyard could stay with the Generals.

On defense, I was supposed to guard Dunbar, who's at least ten inches taller than I am. It was the first time anybody ever dunked on me.

Farrero called time and benched me for the rest of the game. I escaped fully dressed. It's a feat not every guest General can boast.

One General told me that he's played four years and still double knots his pants every game.

Farrero asked me to turn in my uniform. "It's part of the new austerity program."

I used to keep my Generals uniform. But now the Globetrotters are in Chapter 11. "It's not like it used to be," Farrero said.

Except for that losing streak.

Hats and Horns

MADRID—Two years ago, I called my travel agent and asked, "Where is the wildest New Year's Eve celebration in the world?"

Madrid, Spain.

"I want to go."

It was wild, all right, and massive and scary and loud.

One million people, old and young, rich and poor, prostitutes and grandmothers, slightly tipsy and staggering drunk, jammed the Puerto del Sol, the Times Square of Madrid, to hug and kiss and throw cherry bombs at each other.

They come from everywhere to celebrate in Madrid.

"I was visiting Paris on vacation but I flew to Madrid for one night," said an Illinois doctor. "It's something I've heard about and I had to see. It's pretty crazy."

The tradition is to eat grapes at midnight. The big clock on the Direccion General de Seguridad building (police headquarters) strikes twelve gongs. One grape per gong.

Every street corner has a guy selling grapes, neatly counted in plastic bags.

I went to the party prepared. I bought grapes that morning and carefully removed the seeds. I was a tourist and I wasn't going to spit.

I did something smart, too. I left my wallet and passport in my hotel room. I stuffed 3,500 pesetas (about thirty-five dollars when you consider the lousy exchange rate at hotels) in my pocket and took the subway to Puerto del Sol.

Puerto del Sol—that's Spanish for Pickpockets Paradise. My 3,500 pesetas never saw ten p.m. I'm pretty sure the heist occurred when two drunks started fighting and I was pushed to the ground by a surge of amateur boxing fans. The guy who helped me up. I think he got my money. He didn't like the exchange rate at hotels, either.

Firecrackers the size of dynamite sticks filled the night air. Bottle rockets whizzed overhead. Dogs barked. Babies cried. I wondered if this party was on TV back at the hotel.

Madrilenos get very emotional on New Year's Eve. Men kiss men. Women kiss women. They wear ridiculous outfits and do silly dances. It's like being in a Madonna video.

You go where the mob takes you. I walked two blocks and never moved my feet.

At eleven p.m., one million people squeezed into a place that holds about 50,000. Homeowners in West University know the feeling.

It was the loudest sustained noise I ever heard. People just standing there, chugging cheap champagne, and screaming at the top of their lungs. Then they smashed the bottles on the ground.

Huge searchlights, like when a car dealership opens, bounced off buildings. Distinguished Spaniards in expensive clothing mingled with drunk American college kids in sweatpants.

In the middle of the Puerto del Sol, an orchestra played classical music. On a side street, blind men danced for tossed coins.

The local McDonald's was closed, but they lined up for Wendy's. In Madrid, Wendy's hamburgers are round, not square. A double cheeseburger, fries and a Coca-Cola Light cost about eight dollars.

American cigarettes cost four dollars, twice the price of domestic brands.

It's so crowded, you can't see the ground, but you can feel the cigarette butts and broken glass.

At midnight, the Direccion de Seguridad clock sprung into action. A golden ball descended and a shimmering Felize flashed on the roof. Everybody ate grapes.

The noise level, which couldn't get noisier, did. Loudspeakers on city buildings played the Beatles' "All You Need Is Love."

An old lady gave me a hug. I don't like when strangers touch me. Especially the guy who took my 3,500 pesetas.

Either Rich
or Dead

If President Clinton really wants to cut America's health costs, let him check out the back alleys of Southeast Asia.

From Hong Kong to Singapore, and Vietnam in between, I received a bargain-basement, head-to-toe health and beauty makeover that will last me a lifetime.

Unless I caught a bizarre tropical disease from my sixty-cent outdoor dental examination on a side street in Kowloon.

At that price, who needs a ceiling, electricity and diplomas on a wall?

My sudden urge for health started in Hong Kong. I heard about the night market on Temple Road in Kowloon, the nutty side of town.

A travel guide said they have pretty wild junk. The food is greasy and great. But watch out for the fortune tellers and street dentists.

Street dentists?

I found my dentist next to a guy selling socks, five pairs for $3. My dilemma: Argyles or a nice healthy smile? I decided on teeth.

The dentist motioned me to sit. He used a lawn chair. "What can I do for you?"

Tooth extraction was $5. Fillings were $2. Teeth cleaning was $1.

I went for the cleaning and talked him down to sixty cents. It was the first time I ever haggled money with a dentist.

No wonder his prices were so low. He doesn't pay rent. He doesn't have malpractice insurance. He doesn't use sterilized equipment. I seriously doubt if college tuition ever entered the picture.

He kept his tools in a fishing tackle box.

I made him promise not to draw blood. He was gentle. He poked around my teeth with a metal jabber. I rinsed with Diet Pepsi and spit on the sidewalk. Other tourists took my picture.

Two streets over, an old man predicted my future by smelling my bare feet.

I'm gonna be rich!

I proceeded to the outdoor ear acupuncture clinic. A woman, quite possibly a nurse, gave me a total physical examination by sticking a needle in my ears 230 times. Each poke corresponded to a different body part.

Go ahead and laugh, but my small intestine is in horrible shape. My left lung may have to come out. My brain is on its last leg.

The nurse said, "Your brain hurts because you think too much, right? You must learn to relax."

Then she tried to sell me pills guaranteed to help me think less.

I got a haircut on a street in Hanoi for $1. And another one in Saigon for $1. Now I need one in Houston for $20 to even the sides out.

I also got my first manicure in Saigon for $1. The manicurist would have cleaned my ears for $1, but the bus was leaving. Plus my ears were still sore from the physical exam.

In Singapore I had my palm read by a computer for $5.

I'm gonna be rich!

A Good Set
of Choppers

Samson Power is not your ordinary circus strongman.

Let those other strongmen play tug of war with an elephant, stop a racing car dead in its tracks or hoist 1,000-pound barbells over their heads.

Samson lifts stuff with his teeth. Like tables and chairs. And people from the audience. Samson's record so far? He once clamped his choppers on a 410-pound man and spun him around like a rag doll.

Samson does his molar muscleman act every night for the Ringling Bros. and Barnum & Bailey circus. The circus is in town through Sunday at The Summit.

This edition of the Greatest Show on Earth has the usual array of lions and tigers and acrobats and clowns and a woman who hangs from the rafters by her hair. It even has a woman who loads herself onto the world's biggest crossbow and gets shot across The Summit.

But give me a man who lifts fat guys with his teeth.

Samson warms up the audience by chomping down and lifting a fifty-pound table. It looked like mahogany to me. Maybe pine.

Then comes his show-stopper. The spotlight narrows on Samson. The crowd gasps as he plucks a hefty fan from the lower promenade. With drums rolling, he wraps a Velcro belt tightly around the subject's tummy.

Bellowing like a lion, Samson grabs a mouthful of Velcro and hurtles the fan skyward. The audience goes wild. They've never seen anything like this. Samson truly has the "world's strongest teeth."

Surprisingly, Samson began his circus career as a different kind of strongman. Growing up in Mombasa, Kenya, he practiced lifting things with his hair. He started with a small can of water and worked his way up to furniture.

I'm not a talent agent, but if Samson had concentrated on recliners, I could have found him work on Interstate 45 between Tidwell and Parker.

The hair-raising act got him gigs with circuses in Africa and Europe. But he didn't hit the big time, Ringling Bros. and Barnum & Bailey, until he switched to teeth.

Naturally, he's proud of his teeth, which, by the way, are natural. He is missing one lower molar. And he's had a root canal on an upper left tooth. But no false teeth. No bridges. No caps.

His teeth are gleaming white. He's got a dazzling smile.

But are his teeth really in tip-top shape? Is he brushing regularly? Does he floss like he's supposed to? Does Velcro cause tooth decay?

Samson told me he brushes with Aqua Fresh toothpaste. He never eats candy. He keeps his teeth powerful by chewing on nails the size of railroad spikes.

Still, I was worried. So I made an appointment and took Samson to see Dr. Donald Tamborello, dentist to the stars. He's responsible for half the pearly whites you see on Houston TV news.

I recently visited him to get my teeth whitened. Unfortunately I went a little overboard with the bleach, and now I look like Carol Channing.

Dr. Tamborello agreed to give Samson a full dental examination, including x-rays. We met in his office last Friday. The exam was so thorough—all those sharp, poking instruments—that halfway through I asked for nitrous oxide.

After Samson rinsed and spit, Dr. Tamborello gave him the bad news: Start taking better care of your grill or you'll be out of a job in a few years. Then what'll you do? Who's going to pay to watch a circus performer gum a bowl of oatmeal?

"Your overall dental health is not good," he told Samson. "I see evidence of gum disease, especially the uppers. I see root planing and scaling. You need to begin a program of dental care right away."

Even though Ringling Bros. provides dental coverage for its performers, Dr. Tamborello comped Samson on the x-rays and exam.

Samson was so grateful, he picked up Dr. Tamborello with his teeth and spun him around the waiting room.　🌱

No Satisfaction

As assignments go, it's pretty tough to beat this one: Fly to Dallas on Saturday morning, check into a hotel, grab a cab to the Texas Motor Speedway in Fort Worth, watch the Rolling Stones in concert, write a twenty-inch story, file it by 9:30 p.m., then fly home the next day.

A snap, right? Let me tell you about my day.

First I missed my flight—two different ways. I was late because some genius took down the airport exit sign on U.S. 59. So I sort of got lost. When I finally found the airport, it didn't matter, anyway, because I had left my ticket on the kitchen table. I packed my cable TV bill, instead.

Goodbye 9:50 a.m. flight. Hello 1:25 p.m., which allowed me lots of time to sample the reasonably priced snacks at the airport. I would have bought a frozen yogurt, but my mortgage payment is due next week and I don't want to lose the house.

I'm running a few hours behind schedule, but no sweat. The next flight will get me into Dallas at 2:20 p.m. The opening acts don't go on till four p.m. I decided to skip the hotel and go straight from the airport to the Speedway. I'll just lug my suitcase with me.

I hopped in a cab. The driver spoke a language that sounded like Uncle Martin when he didn't want Bill Bixby to know what he was saying on *My Favorite Martian*. From his gestures, I gathered he knew a secret cabbie-only shortcut to the Speedway.

Twenty minutes later, we were stuck in the kind of traffic jam where you just turn off the engine and read a magazine. Nothing was moving except the clock. I was getting worried. Through the magic of charades, I asked how far we were from the Speedway. He said about a mile, maybe a mile and a half.

No sweat. I'll just walk it.

The driver's estimate was about five miles off. I walked for half an hour and still couldn't even see the Speedway. It was getting near show time. I was sweating, not out of nervousness, but from the walking.

Traffic began to inch along and some people in a white pickup truck asked if I wanted a lift. I said sure, and tossed my suitcase in the back of their truck like the Old Spice man and climbed in.

This is what my career has come to. I'm hitchhiking to a rock concert in the back of a truck. Guys on motorcycles were giving me the peace sign and asking if I had extra Rolling Stones tickets.

I made it to the front gate of the Speedway at 4:40 p.m. A female guard went through my bag, you know, in case I was smuggling in a camera or tape recorder.

I said, "No camera. Just deodorant, some underpants and a clean pair of socks. I always bring a complete change of clothes to a rock concert."

Once inside I went to work on my story. I talked to fans, got something to eat, watched the show and soaked up the atmosphere. At seven p.m., I plugged in my Tonka Toy computer that's almost as old as the Rolling Stones and started writing.

At 9:15 I hooked up the computer to a phone, dialed the *Chronicle*, and hit "send."

The computer had a seizure. It made a retching, buzzing noise and the screen went blotto. Paging Dr. Kevorkian! My story had been zapped, suicide-assisted, deleted, gone forever. There was no getting it back.

On top of missing my flight, hitching in the back of a truck and having a strange woman go through my underpants, now I had no story.

That didn't change the fact that I had twenty inches of newspaper space to fill. What appeared in Sunday's paper was me dictating a story off the top of my head, reading notes on pieces of paper stuffed in my pocket and trying to remember what my computer just forgot.

Naturally I blame the Rolling Stones. None of this would have happened if they had performed at the Astrodome instead of that concrete landfill in Fort Worth.

Oy, Dem Slyders

This week I reached out for something a little different: a gigantic box of frozen White Castle hamburgers at Sam's Club. (That explains the gigantic box.)

Ah, the memories. Oh, the nostalgia. Oy, the stomach aches.

That's the trouble with White Castles. It's too easy to eat too many of them.

When I was a little boy, the burgers were twelve cents each. I'd eat a buck's worth, swipe one from my brother and still be hungry. On the plus side, I usually got to stay home from school the next day.

We used to call them Slyders because of their amazing laxative properties. I was surprised to learn that White Castle now also calls them Slyders, because "they're so easy going down."

Well, that's sort of the same thing.

Here's the blueprint: a razor thin, practically bite-sized beef patty, finely chopped onions and a slice of pickle on a steamed two-and-a-half-inch square bun.

Total calories: 140. Fat grams: 12.

Those numbers, remember, are deceptively low. The hamburgers, don't forget, are deceptively small.

The first White Castle was built in 1921 in Wichita, Kan. White Castle claims to be the first fast-food restaurant. Good, now we know where to send the complaint letters.

Decades before McDonald's erected its first golden arch (and Burger King moved in across the street), there was White Castle, its gleaming medieval towers beckoning like the Statue of Liberty. "Give me your tired, your poor, your huddled masses yearning for a greasy, five-cent hamburger."

If you ever visit a White Castle at four a.m., you'll see some huddled masses, all right.

That's how much a White Castle cost back in 1921: a plugged nickel. Today they go for as much as forty-three cents in New York and as low as thirty-eight cents in Dayton, Ohio.

However, Pepto-Bismol is regular price in Dayton, so a midnight munchie run to Ohio is not practical. But if you go, bring me back a dozen burgers.

Despite all the fast-food restaurants crowding the highway, White Castle hamburgers are unique. They are steam-cooked atop a bed of chopped onions. Each hamburger has five holes strategically punched to allow even heat distribution. The burgers are cooked superfast, only on one side.

White Castle hamburgers may be the world's great guilty pleasure. They are incredibly delicious. White Castle's motto is "Buy 'em by the sack" and they aren't kidding.

Now you can buy 'em by the paper sack in your neighborhood supermarket. In some lucky cities, they even have vending machines dispensing White Castle hamburgers. Is technology wonderful, or what?

Unlike Marie Callender's pot pies and Nathan's hot dogs, frozen White Castle hamburgers are the same exact product you get in the restaurants. Oh, sure, the burger may lose a little greasiness and flavor in the flash freezing process, but it's still cheaper than a flight to Dayton.

Tattoo Parade

Aspiring deep-sea diver Colby Lorenz was the grand-prize winner at the 1998 Tattoo Parade Saturday night at Borders Books. Lorenz impressed the judges with some major tattoo work on his back (a naked man deep in thought) and upper thigh (a pioneer in full mountain-man regalia).

In all, Lorenz was sporting about $3,000 worth of tattoos on his body. All over his body. And these were permanent tattoos, not the lick-on kind you get with Bazooka bubble gum.

Lorenz defeated five other contestants who displayed their various tattoos, body piercings and—yikes!—branding.

I judge this event each year because I like how they introduce me to the crowd.

"Our next judge is Ken Hoffman, who's with the *Houston Chronicle*. He doesn't have any tattoos . . . yet."

Lorenz's victory in the tattoo contest was a triumph of love. His wife, Natasha, is a tattoo artist. In fact, that's how they met. She's the one who drew the mountain man on him.

"He kept coming back for more work. Finally I told him he should just ask me out for a date," Natasha said.

Now Colby gets his tattoos for free.

Natasha has five tattoos herself, not counting the single most bizarre tattoo I've ever seen. She rolled down her bottom lip, and there it was: a simple, two-word obscene message in capital letters. The big one.

Now, why would somebody have that tattooed inside her lip?

"It's because of the traffic on the freeway," she said. "When somebody cuts me off, it does no good to yell at them. They can't

195

hear you. But this way I can speed up next to them, press my mouth against the window, and they get the message."

Whatever happened to the old-fashioned hand gesture?

I asked Natasha, "What's the weirdest tattoo you've ever seen, present company excluded? And by present company, I mean your lip."

She said she knew a guy who lost his big toe in an accident. It came clean off. After he healed, on the skin where his big toe used to be, he got a tattoo of a happy face.

My Hero

How many times has this happened?

You pull into the drive-through and order two burgers with just ketchup, large French fries and a Diet Coke. Then you drive away, dig into your bag and find two burgers with everything BUT ketchup, small onion rings and a chocolate shake. Aaargh!

They always nail you in the drive-through.

If I were any kind of a man, you know what I'd do? I'd make a Bat Turn in my nuclear-powered GEO Tracker, screech up to that drive-through and . . . and . . .

But I'm a wimp like everybody else. I meekly wipe the mayonnaise off the burgers, toss the onion rings and chug the chocolate shake. The weird thing is, I'll go back to that same drive-through the next day. And they'll get my order wrong again.

That's why Robert Norsworthy is my hero.

Saturday night, Norsworthy did something I only dream about.

First he yanked on the front door of the Jack in the Box on Wayside. But it was eleven p.m., and the door was locked. Only the drive-through was open. So he went around to the drive-through window, where, of course, they don't serve walk-ups, and . . . and . . .

Norsworthy kicked in the drive-through window and jumped into the Jack in the Box.

That's why he's my hero. (Except for the part where a security guard shot him two times in the side, and he was arrested for trespassing. Now he's in Ben Taub Hospital with a cop outside his door twenty-four hours a day, and he's got to eat that horrible hospital food, and they don't have cable TV.)

Minor details. Come to think of it, I've never liked that rule where you have to be in a car to use the drive-through, either.

Forget the Beatles song "She Came in Through the Bathroom Window."

Somebody should record "Robert Norsworthy Came in Through the Drive-Through Window." It would be Number One with a bullet. Actually two bullets.

Wednesday morning, I visited Norsworthy at Ben Taub. I tried to smuggle in an Ultimate Breakfast Sandwich (two pieces of ham, bacon, cheese and egg on a sesame seed bun . . . delicious) from Jack in the Box, but the cop at the door confiscated it.

Norsworthy said he was feeling "a little better" but didn't know when he is getting out of the hospital. He would have a felt "a lot better" if the cop had let him eat the Ultimate Breakfast Sandwich.

I asked Norsworthy what it felt like to crash through the drive-through window. Did he feel he was getting even for every customer who ever ordered a chicken sandwich and got a fish filet instead?

Norsworthy said it had nothing to do with consumer affairs. He said he was running away from two guys who were chasing him. He jumped through the drive-through for safety. He didn't have a gun on him. It wasn't a stickup.

The security guard's story is that Norsworthy came at him in a threatening manner, so the guard shot him.

That's their stories, and they're sticking to them.

I was after more important stuff. Like, why Jack in the Box? There are tons of fast-food joints in that area.

"I always go to Jack in the Box," Norsworthy said. "I go there almost every day. I'm a regular. You can ask them."

Is it the Sourdough Jack? The new, crispier French fries? The shakes with real ice cream? The two tacos for ninety-nine cents?

"Nah, I don't eat anything there except for the Jumbo Jack. It's really good. It's the best. I like it more than anywhere else," he said.

Norsworthy said he hasn't tried the new fries at Jack in the Box.

I told him they were pretty good, but maybe he should try the new fries at Burger King, too.

But use the front door this time, OK?

Spin Doctor

THE EQUATOR—If the equator ran through America, there'd be a T-shirt shop, waterslide and snack bar directly on latitude zero degrees zero minutes. We'd have Disney Equator World and Trailer Park. Book early and reserve the swanky *Gilligan's Island* suite.

But in Kenya, the equator is barely a pit stop on the bumpy Nanyuki-Isiolo Highway. There isn't even a red light. Just a dinky, unlighted "You are now passing the Equator" sign.

And a high school kid named "Professor Paul" demonstrating the equator's effect on toilet bowls.

It is true that water spins one way down a toilet in the Southern Hemisphere and the opposite direction up north. This is called the "Coriolis Effect," which, on a larger scale, tells ocean currents which way to flow.

If the equator can turn oceans topsy-turvy, it certainly can dictate how a toilet flushes.

They don't have public restrooms along the Nanyuki-Isiolo Highway, so Professor Paul has to improvise the Coriolis Effect.

Tourists walk twenty feet north of the equator. Professor Paul drops a toothpick in a funnel of water. As the water drains, the tooth-pick turns clockwise. Twenty feet south of the equator, darned if the toothpick doesn't turn counter-clockwise. Then Professor Paul conducts the experiment smack on the equator. The water drains straight down. The toothpick doesn't move.

Before the tour bus leaves, Professor Paul hustles his personally autographed "I Crossed The Equator" certificates for $7.

Except for Professor Paul's science class and sales pitch, travelers would never know they're passing Earth's dividing line, where daylight lasts precisely twelve hours every day of the year.

U.S. Navy men know when they cross the equator, though. Especially when it's their first time. That's when they're inducted in the Royal Order of Shellbacks. First timers must eat a concoction of raw eggs, flour, ketchup and last night's leftovers.

If the rookie sailor is lucky, he'll escape with only a shaved head.

"After the ceremony you get a membership card. You don't lose that card because it's proof that you've crossed the equator. You never want to go through that again," said retired fighter pilot Woody Cater of Minneapolis.

What accounts for these hijinks on the high seas? Connecticut physician Marvin Levine said the equator can play tricks on people.

"If you believe that our health is determined by electro-magnetic polarity, anything that upsets that polarity could change our physical character," Levine said.

Ten miles off the highway, at the base of Mount Kenya, the regal Mount Kenya Safari Club straddles the equator. The guest registry reads like a Hollywood wax museum, circa 1965. Yellowing photos of Frank Sinatra and Dean Martin plaster the lobby wall.

The Safari Club tennis court lies directly on the equator. The server stands in the Southern Hemisphere, the receiver in the Northern. I half expected the ball to explode as it crossed the net.

The late actor William Holden founded the Safari Club in 1956 and lived here for twenty-five years. His good friend Stephanie Powers still maintains an orphanage for sick animals on the property.

Some of the Safari Club guest rooms are in the Southern Hemisphere, others in the Northern Hemisphere. Tonight I'm conducting my own experiment. I will go to several rooms on both ends, flush the toilet and see which direction the water spins.

I wonder if Professor Paul needs a partner.

Close Shave

Most American men are Jack the Rippers when it comes to shaving. We're butchers. Cutthroat pirates.

Half of American men shave in the shower, using an old, dull disposable blade and whatever shave cream happened to be on sale at the supermarket.

Once the mirror fogs up, we shave by Braille. The water going down the drain looks like the shower scene from *Psycho*.

Gary Stevens, master barber of the exclusive Geo. F. Trumper shop in London, was in Houston last week to teach us heathens the proper, gentlemanly way to shave. He ought to know. Stevens is Prince Charles's personal groomer.

Stevens also was here to introduce Geo. F. Trumper shaving accessories and cosmetics for men at Bill Walker Clothier on Post Oak. It's the only store in Houston that sells the Trumper line.

Bright and early last Wednesday, I got the royal treatment. Stevens shaved me just like he shaves Prince Charles. Except the tip was probably a lot smaller.

First Stevens wanted to know my normal shaving habits.

I'm in the fiftieth percentile that doesn't shave in the shower. I lather up and let it sit on my face for about ten minutes while I do other things around the house. Sometimes I talk on the phone, which is a treat for the next person who makes a call. They get an earful of shaving cream.

I use Bic disposable razors, the yellow ones for sensitive skin.

I shave as fast as I can. I usually scrape my neck pretty badly. My towel looks like Prosecution Exhibit A from the O.J. Simpson trial.

Every guy has a trouble spot. Mine is right under my nose at the nostril-upper lip border. I can't squeeze the razor under there without becoming a blood donor.

Stevens looked at me and just shook his head.

He covered my face with a steaming hot towel, like you get in first class on an airplane. This was to open my pores. Then he massaged Coral Skin Food into my face to soothe my abused skin.

No more cheap shaving foam from a can. You need to buy a brush and quality cream. On me, he used a rose-scented, glycerine-based cream. He worked the lather into my face and let it sit for a few minutes.

If this were my usual barber shop, this would be the time I'd stare at the barber's license taped to the mirror, then at the person cutting my hair, and see if they're even remotely the same person.

Having someone else shave me was incredibly relaxing.

I've always thought the best part of getting a haircut is the shampoo. If they throw in a quickie shoulder rub, that's the bonus plan.

If somebody opened a barber shop called Just Shampoos, they'd become billionaires.

Stevens lathered me up a second time, which I didn't think was necessary. He's been reading too many shampoo bottles.

He used a $500 brush made from badger hair, a Warwick razor and a Gillette Sensor blade.

Stevens shaved me closer than an accountant looking for dinner receipts.

"Always shave with the grain. Down on your face, up on your neck. If you go in the wrong direction you'll get razor burn and ingrown hairs," he said.

Stevens used a small bowl of warm water to wash off the razor. At home I leave the faucet running and waste 100,000 gallons of hot water. People look at my water bill and think I own a swimming pool.

He asked what kind of cologne I wanted.

I normally don't use cologne. I leave the house "as is." So I said, "Give me the same stuff Prince Charles uses."

That would be Extract of Limes. The Prince orders twelve bottles, each month. I asked who could use that much cologne?

"We always used to wonder about that ourselves," Stevens said. "Then we discovered that Prince Charles was splashing some in his bath water. But one thing about him, he's a charming fellow, and he always returns his empty bottles." ❦

Trunks Up!

NAIROBI, KENYA—While the rest of our group is having dinner in a swanky hotel restaurant, I'm sneaking off to Nairobi's most notorious nightclub.

The Modern Twenty-four Hour Green Bar is world-class insanity. It's the crummiest bar on a crummy street in a bad part of town. *The Lonely Planet Guide to Kenya* describes the Modern Green as "an unparalleled spit and sawdust binge."

All human life congregates here: tourists with cameras around their necks, teen girls chewing miraa (stimulating roots), ladies of the evening, con artists, the filthy rich and dirt poor, and lowlifes of all ages and races.

"It's definitely not for the squeamish," *Lonely Planet* warns.

This is my kind of place—the seamier the better.

The Modern Green opened in 1970 and has been closed only one day since, back in 1989, so they could take the national census.

The bar boasts a super-charged jukebox that blares African reggae at ear-shattering decibels. It never shuts off. Customers are packed like claustrophobic sardines and a bartender works inside a wire cage for his own protection.

You can spot the tourists. They're the ones dressed in African dashikis and animal charm necklaces. You can tell the Kenyans just as easily. They're wearing Chicago Bull T-shirts and L.A. Raider caps.

The bartender's cage has a hole the size of a fist. Customers pass money through it. Beer comes out the other way.

A twenty-ounce bottle of Tusker, Africa's premium brew, costs one dollar. The label shows an elephant in full charge. When a Kenyan hoists a Tusker, the popular toast is "Trunks up!"

A glass of Changaa on tap, the foul local stuff, costs only thirty cents. "Two glasses and you fall over blind," said bartender Samuel Chege Kanyuire.

The Modern Green has a full service kitchen in back. The chef's choice is Githeri, a steaming mound of corn, beef, potatoes mixed together in a creamy sauce.

Fighting is not allowed at the Modern Green, but they have lots of fights. Robbery isn't allowed, either, but watch your wallet. Especially in the bathrooms.

It's hard to tell the pickpockets from the prostitutes. This is a very touchy-feely crowd. I was mauled and grabbed more than an Oilers quarterback.

On the wall, in Swahili, is a sign:

"Juz ilikkuwa kukopa: Jana vile vile, Led lipa cash las Sivyo ura."

It means, "Yesterday was credit, today you pay cash or get lost."

The Modern Green is jammed at all hours, all day. Three a.m. on a torrential Tuesday? Packed.

"This is the most famous bar in Kenya because of the walk-in tourists from all over the world," Kanyuire said. "They go home, they tell their friends, and they come here, too. It's a crazy group, I tell you."

The Modern Green opened as a daytime-only bar in 1970. It went twenty-four hours in 1974 after extensive remodeling. It's one of the few bars in Kenya that's allowed to stay open all night.

The wildest night is Friday.

"Friday is payday and everybody can relax tomorrow. So they really let loose. You cannot move inside and the party spills out onto the street," Kanyuire said.

The walls rattle from the jukebox. Five cents will get you three songs. Children smoke unfiltered cigarettes. A soupy cloud of smoke hovers near the ceiling at seven p.m. By midnight it reaches the floor.

It's hot, sweaty and stinky. Your clothes reek of cigarette smoke and beer stains.

"You never know who comes in. The mayor is a regular customer. We're so popular because people have fun. Sometimes they have so much fun that I have to call the police," Kanyuire laughed.

She *Is* a
World Champion

I tried to have an open mind about the WNBA, the new women's pro basketball league. But every time I tuned in a game, I saw a demolition derby.

Players wildly knocked into each other. They heaved bricks like new construction in Cinco Ranch. There were more turnovers than at Three Brothers Bakery.

They can't shoot. They can't dribble. They can't dunk. Some league this is. Houston's No.1 draft choice missed training camp because she was pregnant.

These are professional basketball players? Give me a break. I'm strictly a backyard bomber and I can beat their best players one-on-one. That's what I thought.

So I called, "I got next."

And I got whacked.

My opponent was Kim Perrot, starting point guard for the Houston Comets. Kim has some impressive numbers on the back of her Topps trading card. During her senior year at the University of Southwestern Louisiana, she led the nation in scoring with a 30.0 average. She once scored fifty-eight points against arch-rival Southeastern Louisiana.

After college, she played pro ball in France, Israel and Sweden. In Israel, she averaged twenty-five points a game, so she's had experience whipping up on my people.

But here's the only stat I cared about. Kim is only five feet five inches tall. She's a shrimp in high-top Nikes.

I'm a strapping lad of almost six feet (on a good hair day). This will be a snap. I'll do the Gene Peterson bit, "Backing in, backing in, backing in," and shoot lay-ups all day.

Anyway, this wouldn't be the first time I've played a female pro basketballer. A few years ago, the Harlem Globetrotters came to Houston with Lynette Woodard on their roster. I played a few minutes for the other team, the sad-sack Washington Generals. I guarded Woodard.

All I remember from that night was Globetrotter legend Louis Dunbar trying to pull down my pants on the foul line. And me trying to remember if I wore boxer shorts.

I wasn't worried about Kim de-pantsing me. I certainly wasn't concerned about her blocking my shot. I'm used to playing tall, manly guys on the unforgiving asphalt of inner-city West University. These guys are animals.

Before I tell you exactly how Kim wiped the floor with me, allow me four lame excuses.

1. Earlier that day I was painting the inside of my house. I was goofy on Dutch Boy fumes.

2. The official WNBA ball is smaller than I figured. I've eaten bigger cantaloupes.

3. I stopped by McDonald's on the way over.

4. I'm pregnant.

The rules were: We would play one game to fifteen. Baskets count one point. Shots from behind the three-point line count two points.

Kim shot dead or alive and missed. I took the ball out. My brilliant strategy worked like a charm. I shoved my rear end out and backed in for a layup. Kim got the ball and nailed a two-pointer. I hit another layup. She hit another two-pointer.

Some brilliant strategy. I made four shots in a row and was losing 8-4.

I couldn't guard her long-range missiles. She was too fast. She dribbled between her legs and behind her back. This wasn't like playing my pasty accountant buddies in West U. Those weenies.

Kim ran me into the ground. When she got ahead, I was forced to abandon the lay-ups. Unfortunately, I couldn't make a long shot. The pint-sized ball messed me up. (Excuse No. 2.)

I was feeling a little queasy, too. (Excuse No. 3, possibly No. 4). When the score hit 14-10, I gave up. "Here, hit another two-pointer and put me out of my misery."

She did. Game over, 16-10. Kim missed maybe two shots the whole game. So I have new-found respect for the Houston Comets and the whole WNBA. From now on, I'm a hoopster feminist.

And the next time KILT's talk host Rich Lord says, "Comet is something you clean the kitchen sink with," I'm going to call in and set him straight.

Top Ten Degrees

Manhattan—Cameras are set to roll in fifteen minutes on *The Late Show With David Letterman*, and staff writer Bill Scheft is "warming up" an audience that desperately needs some warming up.

It's awfully cold inside the Ed Sullivan Theatre, where Letterman tapes his talk show in New York. You can see your breath.

"It's about fifty-four degrees in here," a CBS page said. "That's usually the first question everybody asks."

It's chilly on purpose. According to a Letterman spokesman, cool temps translate to alert audiences.

The Letterman show tapes at 5:30 p.m. for airing that same night after the late local news.

Fans who write for tickets (they're free) face an eight-month wait. Or you can take a chance and hang around the theater, hoping a ticket-holder doesn't show. But get there early. The line begins forming at seven a.m.

If there's a particularly heavy-duty guest, Madonna, for example, fans camp out overnight.

Recorded rock music blares as the audience enters single file into the 800-seat theater. "Don't skip any seats," the ushers say.

Scheft starts his warm-up at 5:10 p.m. He carries a big, unlit cigar and paces the stage like Alan King on the original *Ed Sullivan Show*. Another Letterman writer says, "Bill's in his thirties, but he has the heart and soul of a seventy-year-old comic."

"Hey, howya doin'?" Scheft hollers. "The theater has been air-conditioned for your discomfort."

He lays down three rules:

1) Don't yell out personal messages to Letterman. "This isn't a Jets game."

2) Don't wave at the camera. "You'll look like a bigger yutz than Andrew Giuliani."

3) No standing ovations and definitely no barking (like Arsenio Hall's audience). "If you bark, a page will take you outside and have you neutered."

Scheft introduces a funny video of Letterman and bandleader Paul Shaffer playing golf that aired several months ago. Then he roars, "Whaddya say we bring out the band?"

The musicians are introduced one at a time, Shaffer last. They crank up "Dance To The Music," by Sly and the Family Stone.

With three minutes to taping, Letterman walks out, in shirt and tie, to welcome the audience and present one audience member with a treasured prize—a canned ham.

"Where do you get your hair cut?" someone hollers.

"What's it to you?" Letterman asks. Finally he admits, "I go to Riker's Island once a month."

Riker's Island is home to a large prison in New York.

Letterman retreats backstage for his sports jacket while announcer Bill Wendell announces the night's guests. The audience cannot hear Wendell.

The show rolls along exactly as you see it at home. There are no intermissions, no stops to fix things and no do-overs.

During commercials, the band plays soul hits and Letterman is descended upon by writers, producers, stage managers and a make-up artist. Letterman rarely talks to his guests during commercials.

After the last commercial, Letterman bids good night to his guest and thanks the audience for coming. "Come back soon," he says.

Letterman beats the guest offstage by several feet. In two minutes, the audience is cleared out.

To go home and watch the show. Again. And wait another eight months for tickets.

Touring Hell-ywood

HOLLYWOOD—What I wanted to do was take a tour of the stars' homes in Hollywood. But my incompetent friend Elliot Segal, who swore he knew where all the big shots lived, could do no better than find Nanette Fabray's house. "See that big wall? Well, right behind it is the house they used on the *Beverly Hillbillies*," he said.

"Elliot, take me back to the hotel," I said. "I should have taken the geeky sightseeing bus."

But Elliot had another idea. "How about the Hell Tour of Hollywood? This place is the capital of disgusting things. If you like bizarre, I can show you where it happened."

I hopped back in the car. For three hours, Elliot pointed to places where murder, suicide and all sorts of human craziness took place.

Elliot will never work for the Chamber of Commerce.

The Hell Tour started at 6315 Hollywood Blvd., the site of the original Sardi's restaurant. During the thirties and forties, all the big stars came to Sardi's for corned beef sandwiches. Sardi's was Charlie Chaplin's favorite hangout. Now it's a porno theater.

Farther down Hollywood Boulevard, we passed the Mortuary of the Stars. That's the actual name of the place. Actress Peg Entwhistle had her funeral services here. She is the only person to commit suicide by jumping off the famous "Hollywood" sign.

You really need a whole day to see the Hollywood Memorial Cemetery. But if you're only driving by, visit Section Eight-Outside. That's where Our Gang star Carl "Alfalfa" Switzer is buried. He was shot to death in 1959 in an argument over $50. He was thirty-three.

Mel Blanc's nearby gravestone reads, "That's all folks!"

We drove to East Hollywood, to 1731 N. Normandie, where actor

Albert Dekker was found dead. Dekker is best known for his role as Dr. Cyclops in the movies.

In 1968, police discovered Dekker's body in the bathroom of his small apartment. He was dangling from a rope around his neck. Another rope tied up both his legs and one arm. His hands were handcuffed behind his back. Two hypodermic needles were stuck in his body.

Police originally listed his death as suicide. Later the coroner reported his death as "an accident."

We drove to 1822 Camino Palermo, Ozzie and Harriet's old home in the Hollywood Hills. Ricky and David grew up in this house.

Ozzie died in 1975, and Harriet lived there alone until she sold the place in 1980. The new owners started noticing strange things, like faucets turning on by themselves and lights blinking. The family has only one explanation—the house is haunted by the ghost of Ozzie!

We took a break at C.C. Brown's ice cream shop at 7007 Hollywood Blvd. This is where the hot fudge sundae was invented. Nobody was ax murdered here or anything. I just love hot fudge sundaes.

Janis Joplin died of a drug overdose in 1970 at the Landmark Hotel, 7047 Franklin Ave. Joplin had set aside money for her own wake. The Grateful Dead entertained. Invitations read, "The drinks are on Pearl."

John Matuszak died of a heart attack in 1989 in his home at 3429 Oak Glen. Inger Stevens took an overdose in 1970 at 8000 Woodrow Wilson Drive.

Marilyn Monroe was found dead in 1962 at 12305 Fifth Helena Drive. A few streets over, at 426 N. Bristol, is where Joan Crawford yelled, "No more wire hangers," at her daughter.

West Hollywood is one huge crime scene. Here is where Sal Mineo was knifed in 1976 on the Sunset Strip. John Belushi overdosed in bungalow No. 2 of the Chateau Marmont, 8221 Sunset Blvd., in 1982. In 1977, Comedian Freddie Prinze killed himself in his apartment at 865 Comstock.

Many film historians consider Florence Lawrence as America's first movie star. In 1910, she became the first actress whose name was listed in a movie's credits. She also was the first actress to sign a movie contract.

In 1938, depressed and forgotten, she committed suicide by swallowing ant paste. Her home still stands at 532 Westbourne. 🌿

Beyond Trash TV

SECAUCUS, NJ—As things go, this was a pretty uneventful taping of *The Richard Bey Show*.

Only five police cars were called to break up fights among audience members.

The Richard Bey Show is television's newest, trashiest, fur-flyingest, most bizarre daytime talk show. If Oprah is trying to take the high road, then Bey is tunneling beneath Death Valley. He should hit China any day now.

The bushy-eyebrowed host, who shot to national prominence hosting Juiceman infomercials, wonders aloud, "Where do they get these people?"

Richard, it's your show, you don't know?

Tuesday's subject was "My girlfriend wants to be a stripper, but I'll dump her if she does." The guests were all in their teens. In New Jersey and New York, you have to be at least twenty-one to be a stripper.

Only a minor detail.

Before the show I met Bobby, one of the unhappy boyfriends who are "flipping because their girlfriends want to be stripping." Bobby was sent back to the Green Room to get rid of his hooded sweatshirt. He wasn't a happy unhappy boyfriend.

"I don't want to be here. This started out as a joke. I called the phone number they gave on TV as a joke. I never thought they'd want us on the show," Bobby said. "They want me to jump through a window and hit my girlfriend with a pie. That's stupid. I won't do it."

Most daytime talk shows are based in glamorous Manhattan,

with theater marquees as elaborate as Broadway plays.

The Richard Bey Show tapes Monday through Friday at WWOR-TV in sooty, blue-collar Secaucus. Giants Stadium and the Meadowlands complex are about a mile away. It's a rough area.

The Green Room, where guests wait for the show to begin, had a stain-soaked carpet, an empty box of supermarket doughnuts and a half-filled cup of cold coffee spiked with cigarette butts.

The studio audience, mostly young and totally loud, filed in about 4:45 p.m. It seemed like everybody was there because, "I know one of the people on the stage."

Bey bopped out at five p.m. to greet the audience. The crowd stomped and hooted and waved their arms in Arsenio Hall "woof woof" fashion.

"Thanks for the applause . . . but it's not good enough," Bey said. "I want you to clap like Madonna, Snoop Doggy Dogg and Barbra Streisand were here!"

Uh, who's that last one, Richard?

The stripper wannabes were seated onstage covered with green bed sheets. The disapproving boyfriends were introduced one at a time, each leveling a threat of abandonment.

Meanwhile, a ruckus was breaking out between two guys in the row behind me.

It was one of those arguments where I heard every word and I still have no idea what they were fighting about.

Maybe they couldn't agree which one had more earrings through his nose.

Onstage, things were getting hot. Bey removed the bed sheets from the girls like he was unveiling statues in the park.

A female audience member chided one of the boyfriends: "Can't you control your girlfriend? Did you hear what she just said? You should hit her."

The argument behind me was inching closer to a fist fight.

So was the ruckus onstage. Bey Show stagehands prodded them

with signs scribbled in markers saying, "Argue!" and "Louder" and "Speak up!"

No lawsuits resulted from Monday's taping. The head of security said the show had three lawsuits pending, though, including two guests suing each other over an onstage slap-fight.

Everybody in the audience has to pass through a metal detector. Monday they confiscated one knife. Guests have to go through the metal detector, too, especially since the time a guest hacked up a leather couch in the Green Room.

During the second half of the show, Bey introduced an evangelical ex-stripper and a cop who encourages young people to walk the straight and narrow.

The cop warned one girl, you know, if you become a stripper your boyfriend might look up an old girlfriend.

"Oh, no, he won't, 'cause she's a dirty, yeast-infected skank," she said.

The ex-stripper sat in the seat directly in front of me. She warned girls that dancing in a topless club was a dead end life. She said she's suffered from drug and alcohol abuse, anorexia and bulimia and low self-esteem. She also said she'd had six abortions.

Now she works for an advertising agency. She hopes it's a step up.

The show ended with one of the underage girls making her stripping debut. Well, she almost made her stripping debut but right before she got to undressing, her boyfriend (not Bobby) pelted her with custard pies.

Bey thanked the audience for coming. On the way out, the security guard returned a pocket knife to one of the guys fighting behind me.

Five minutes later, this same guy was throwing fists in the parking lot.

Enter the cops. A squadron of Secaucus' finest was summoned to break up the melee.

When the dust settled, the security guard shrugged his shoulders, hopped into his car and rolled down a window.

"Just another day in the life of *The Richard Bey Show*," he laughed. "I miss the good old peaceful days . . . when I worked on the *Morton Downey Jr. Show*."

Hold the Anchovies!

I never had a Caesar's salad until about a year ago. Now I love 'em. In fact, Caesar's salad is closing the gap on pizza as my all-time favorite dish. A good Caesar's is delicious, filling and usually cheap.

So I took a pilgrimage, down to Old Tijuana, to Caesar's Grill and Hotel on Fifth and Main. I went to the kitchen where this blend of romaine lettuce, Parmesan cheese, a dash of Worcestershire, salt and pepper, croutons, garlic-flavored oil, vinegar, a raw egg and lemon juice was invented.

Like most essentials of life, Caesar's salad was created out of necessity. Caesar's Grill and Hotel was built in the early 1920s by an Italian businessman named Caesar Cardini. It was small, with nineteen rooms and a modest dining room.

Each Sunday, Cardini traveled to market in San Diego, where food supplies were cheaper and fresher than in Mexico. He bought an entire week's worth of groceries.

During the Roaring Twenties, Tijuana was a jumping city. Only 30,000 or 40,000 people lived there. But on weekends, "The Most Visited City In The World" turned party town. With Prohibition the law in the United States, Californians would dip South of the Border and eat, drink and be merry. Mostly drink.

On July 4, 1925, after a particularly busy week, Caesar's Grill ran out of food. Resourceful Cardini took a huge bowl, tossed in some lettuce, a few eggs, olive oil . . ..A legend was born.

So it is Caesar's salad, not Caesar salad. It's named for an Italian restaurateur in Mexico, not some Roman emperor with a Beatle haircut and untrustworthy friends.

Cardini sold the hotel and restaurant in 1938, moved to Los

Angeles and opened a gourmet food store. His top seller? "Cardini's Famous Caesar's Salad Dressing" in a bottle. You can still buy it.

Here is where you'd expect to read that Caesar's salad was an instant hit. But it wasn't.

"The original Caesar's salad had olive oil. People did not like that," said Antonio Espericuata, captain of Caesar's Grill and a fifty-year veteran of tossin' salads in Tijuana. "A few years later, we changed from using olive oil. Now we tell people they can use any oil except olive oil."

There have been other, less critical, changes.

It used to be that Espericuata, a dapper man in tuxedo, personally prepared your Caesar's salad table side. It was like a floor show. Today a waiter brings them ready-made from the kitchen.

Caesar's Grill doesn't keep secrets. They use Mazola corn oil and Lea and Perrin's Worcestershire sauce, both straight from a supermarket around the corner.

Like Tijuana, Caesar's Grill and Hotel has done some expanding over the years. Tijuana bulges with two million people today. The hotel now has seventy rooms. The restaurant invites tourists with a sign, "Home Of The Original Caesar's Salad."

The main attraction costs $3.95. But Caesar's Grill regards Caesar's salad like McDonald's does French fries. It goes with everything else on the menu.

Now is a good time to discuss anchovies—those vile menaces to the pizza industry, those salty creatures that must be hunted down and removed from a Caesar's salad.

Espericuata's face crinkles at the mention of the foul fish.

"Oh, no, a true Caesar's salad does not have anchovies. I do not know why Americans put them in. We do not do that. We have never done that," he said.

Espericuata also doesn't know where America got the idea to serve Caesar's salad with a chilled fork, either. "Why do you do that? Do you also serve soup with a hot spoon?"

Pizza Pilgrimage

NAPLES—While my buddies went to the Vatican, I hopped a train south for my own religious experience in noisy Naples.

Naples, the polluted, corrupt, purse-snatching, traffic-jamming, street-walking, horn-honking, firecracker-tossing center of Italy. Naples is where history's first case of syphilis was recorded in 1495.

This is where you get in a cab, and forty-five minutes later, get out, only five blocks from where you started. Housewives scream out the window while drivers lean on their horns while children lob cherry bombs at gridlocked cars.

Forty percent of Naples is unemployed. An epidemic of cholera hit the city in 1973. That's when the world discovered there weren't any sewers in Naples.

Europe's only active volcano, Mount Vesuvius, simmers fifteen miles south of Naples. It last erupted in 1944, coating the city in ash and costing untold millions in improvements.

But I didn't go to Naples for the craziness. I went for pizza. Naples is the home of pizza. The Mecca of mozzarella. The birthplace of basil. The capital of crust. This is where it all started.

I love pizza. I'm not particularly choosy, either. I'll take it thick crust, thin crust, hand-tossed, deep-dish, French bread, whole wheat, loaded with sausage and green peppers. Anything except frozen.

My dream is to own a pizzeria and have my private table in the back near the pinball machine.

In Naples, they swear that Italy's first pizza was made at the Antica Pizzeria on Via Port Alba. From the train station, the Antica is only a half-hour walk (two hours by taxi). It would have been only a half-hour, too, if I hadn't stopped for an Italian hot dog. That's a giant hot dog and greasy French fries stuffed inside a fried doughnut. I may sell these in my pizzeria, too.

Antica Pizzeria is two floors, both of which smell fabulous. The sign outside says *"160 anni di tradizione."* I grabbed a table upstairs. I asked the waiter, is this really the oldest pizzeria in Italy?

"No . . . *in mundo.*"

Skoo-zee? In the world ?

"Si . . . in the world!"

I felt I was in a holy place. I didn't know whether to bow my head or kiss the waiter's ring. This was the pizza purist's pot of gold, the Garden of Eden. When the bible of pizza is written, the Antica Pizzeria will be in the Book of Genesis. Delicious!

I ordered my usual, a large Margherita pizza and a bottle of aqua minerale, no gas.

A little pizza history: The Margherita pizza was invented in the 19th century to honor Margherita di Savoia, the queen of Italy. It seems queenie was visiting Naples, so the cook concocted a special dish just for her. He took the colors of Italy, green basil, white mozzarella and red tomato sauce, and dumped them on round dough.

Mikey liked it! She even allowed the restaurant to use her name on the menu, like the Henny Youngman pastrami combo at a good Jewish delicatessen.

Today you can order a Margherita pizza for 4,000 lire, about $3.60.

The cheapest pizza is the marinara pie for 3,000 lire. Marinara pizza is tomato sauce, laced with spices and powerful chunks of garlic. Be careful, though. This is exactly the combination that caused Vesuvius to explode.

Pizza is different in Italy. Four people don't order one pizza four different ways, like in America. That never works, because the onions and anchovies inevitably invade territory supposedly restricted for pepperoni and mushrooms.

In Italy, everybody gets his own crispy, thin-crust pizza, usually baked in a wood-burning oven.

It's much simpler. Everybody gets more pizza and it usually winds up costing less. I had a pizza delivered last week in Houston that cost $16.99. I looked in the street for a Brinks truck. 🌵

All That Glistens

This week I reached out for a big scoopful of Crumblies at Long John Silver's fried fish emporium.

In case you never knew the proper name for them, Crumblies are left over bits of grease-dripping batter lumps that Long John's sprinkles on top of its fried fish platters.

Here's the blueprint: When Long John Silver's cooks up its fish, they toss some extra batter into the deep fryer. The batter bubbles and breaks into tiny pieces, which are ladled out and aged like a fine wine under an infrared heat lamp.

The Crumblies glisten, all oily and golden brown, like George Hamilton getting ready for another guest shot on "The Tonight Show."

Total calories and fat grams: unknown. Since Crumblies are tossed on for good measure, for free, Long John Silver's doesn't have the nutritional information. Nobody's ever asked before.

Crumblies are the size, shape and color of those 100 percent bran buds you should be eating for breakfast. Bran buds are naturally good for you. They provide essential fiber and vitamins.

Crumblies are unnaturally horrible for you. They provide nothing, except a howling stomach ache if you eat too many of them. They also have an amazing burp shelf life. A good six hours after dinner, Crumblies are still with you, if you catch my drift.

You'll be smart not to catch my drift, however.

On a positive note, Crumblies are very shiny. I've found that shiny food usually tastes good. In proper lighting, pancake syrup can be quite dazzling.

The best part of Crumblies is, just when you think you're done eating and you're about to crinkle up the paper bag, you discover a runaway colony of Crumblies clinging for dear life on the bottom of the sack. It's like you're on a game show and you've made it to the bonus round.

Crumblies taste wonderful. They're everything good about fried food, with none of the nutrition. I tear into Crumblies like Mike Tyson noshing on an ear.

Forget a spoon. Just grab those morsels with your fingers, open wide and insert. Fortunately, Crumblies stick to anything, so you can grab every last one. No offense, Colonel Sanders, but this is finger-lickin' good.

In fact, when I visit Long John Silver's, I wish I could forget the fish altogether and just buy a fifty-five-gallon drum of Crumblies. One time I tried doing that, but the dazed salesperson wouldn't do it. He couldn't figure out how much to charge me. I was about to explain that anything multiplied by zero is still zero when the guy behind me in the drive-through started honking. I changed my order to a fish sandwich and got the heck out of there.

Index